PRIVATIZATION AND PUBLIC HOSPITALS

CHOOSING WISELY FOR NEW YORK CITY

CHARLES BRECHER
SHEILA SPIEZIO

A TWENTIETH CENTURY FUND REPORT

1995 ♦ TWENTIETH CENTURY FUND PRESS ♦ NEW YORK

The Twentieth Century Fund sponsors and supervises timely analyses of economic policy, foreign affairs, and domestic political issues. Not-for-profit and nonpartisan, the Fund was founded in 1919 and endowed by Edward A. Filene.

Library of Congress Cataloging-in-Publication Data

Brecher, Charles.
    Privatization and Public Hospitals: Choosing Wisely for New York City : a report prepared for the Twentieth Century Fund / by Charles Brecher and Sheila Spiezio.
        p. cm.
    Includes index.
    ISBN 0–87078–371–8 (alk. paper)
    1. New York City Health and Hospitals Corporation.   2. Privatization--New York (N.Y.)   I. Spiezio, Sheila.   II. Title.
    RA982.N49B745   1995
    362.1'097471--dc20   95-11195
                                                                                          CIP

Cover Design and Illustration: Claude Goodwin.
Manufactured in the United States of America.

FOREWORD

American politics in 1995 seems to have one overarching theme: get government off the backs of people. Americans have had it pounded into them that their government is, if not the source of all evil, at least a major contributor to just about everything that is wrong. This explanation of what ails us is not merely the stuff of right-wing radio talk show hosts; it is the common fare of our popular culture, including movies, television, and increasingly, print journalism.

In this environment, politicians of every political flavor are leading the charge against the very governments they serve. In New York City as elsewhere, the favored remedy is to privatize anything that can be sold or handed off to profit-seeking businesses.

What seems to have been forgotten in this drive to get rid of costly public "businesses" is that many of these important services, such as subways and commuter railroads, are public precisely because private investors found that they could not operate them at a profit. Should we now shut them down? True, there are some public services that might be profitable if access were restricted to those who could pay full freight. Central Park, Stuyvesant High School, Jones Beach, and the Statue of Liberty might all command handsome prices. But what sort of community would be left if we privatized them?

A generation or two ago, most New Yorkers took public services like CUNY, the New York Public Library, Bellevue Hospital, and Peter Cooper Village for granted; and many took advantage of them. But today, for a large segment of modern New Yorkers, privatization is already well under way. The problems that have made life tougher for all New Yorkers have led lawyers, bankers, executives, and other high-income families to deal with the decline in public services by privatizing on their own. Their children go to private schools. Their residences and favorite restaurants pay for special refuse collection. They have private security in their buildings—and even in their neighborhoods. They rely on black car or limousine service for transportation. They depend on private health insurance and private hospitals. For those who can afford it, the private purchase of formerly public services has become routine.

In addition, many social services have been contracted out to non-governmental—but also nonprofit—agencies. There is widespread agreement that the idea of throwing more public services into a market environment should be explored. It is worth repeating that the advantages of the marketplace are a consequence of the existence of competitive markets (the source of the efficiency gains) and the availability of reasonably complete information, which allows consumers to make informed choices. Moreover, markets work best when entrepreneurs and investors can earn a profit.

In the pages that follow, Charles Brecher and Sheila Spiezio consider the merits of privatizing one of the most expensive and most visible public services provided by New York City: its uniquely extensive public hospital system. The issues raised by health care delivery in the city are enormously complex. Real reform should emerge from a keen sense of current needs and the history behind the development of the current arrangements.

The final section of this report provides the essential background for understanding the factors and events that led to the present structure of the Health and Hospitals Corporation that controls these public institutions. In addition the rapid evolution of health care, including important changes in private insurance programs, the growth of HMOs, and the continuing likelihood of alterations in federal programs such as Medicaid complicate the task of restructuring here and elsewhere.

The authors also point out that, while still meeting the obligation of providing access to health care for the poor, it is entirely possible that the number of facilities now in operation could be reduced. They assert the importance of establishing that the means first be found to pay the private sector to pick up the slack. The authors are tough-minded about privatization, judging it finally not in terms of political power bases or hot campaign slogans, but rather asking how it can be justified, in this case, on the merits. In general, they are negative about privatization only when they conclude that there is simply a good chance that it will not deliver the goods: higher quality for lower cost without reneging on the commitment to care for the indigent.

Decisions about health care have to be different from other, cost/benefit-driven analyses of public versus private systems—different because most of us still claim America is shaped by values, including caring for the less fortunate. In this sense, health care reform is about easing pain and saving lives, not merely about downsizing government and saving money.

Finally, for all the power of our market-driven economy and all the good reasons that we favor it, the authors remind us that it should not be the sole determinant of what we, as a society, do or don't do. Nor should it be seen as the only mechanism that produces good results. When it comes to public health care, the imperatives of political responsiveness and public accountability, as well as the dictates of professional standards and personal principles (in this case those of the medical professional) are often more than a match for the results produced by the pursuit of profit.

On behalf of the Twentieth Century Fund, I thank Charles Brecher and Sheila Spiezio for clarifying the issues involved in privatizing public hospitals in New York City.

RICHARD C. LEONE, *President*
The Twentieth Century Fund
May 1995

CONTENTS

ACKNOWLEDGMENTS

The preparation of this report was made possible by the cooperation of the Citizens Budget Commission, a nonpartisan civic organization devoted to influencing constructive change in the finances and services of New York City and New York State government. The commission, chaired by Lawrence B. Buttenwieser, approved the arrangements for Charles Brecher and Sheila Spiezio to spend part of their time on this project; its Municipal Services Committee, chaired by Bud Gibbs, provided helpful suggestions as part of its review and endorsement of the report on behalf of the commission. The other members of the Municipal Services Committee are Anne Alexander, Harold I. Berliner, Bernard R. Bober, Mark Brossman, Paul Dickstein, Patsy Glazer, Daniel J. Gross, Peter C. Hein, Jerome E. Hyman, William Keller, Christian McCarthy, William F. McCarthy, Frank J. McLoughlin, Bernard H. Mendik, Frances Milberg, Philip L. Milstein, Steven M. Polan, Adam R. Rose, Edward L. Sadowsky, Lee S. Saltzman, Irwin Schneiderman, Barbara Z. Shattuck, Kevin T. Smyley, Ronald G. Weiner, Eileen S. Winterble, and Lawrence B. Buttenwieser, ex-officio.

1.

INTRODUCTION AND OVERVIEW

The winds of change are blowing fiercely in New York. In 1993, the city's residents elected their first Republican mayor since 1965, and in 1994, voters in the state selected their first Republican governor in a generation. These two new leaders each confront fiscal problems as serious as those that arose during the crisis of the late 1970s. By both inclination and necessity, these leaders are raising questions about the scale of government and the most efficient ways to accomplish public purposes. Moreover, the results of the 1994 congressional elections are intensifying the pressures on state and local officials to cut expenditures and restructure government operations.

Not surprisingly, there are loud and frequent cries for "privatization." The purpose of this paper is to analyze the relevance of privatization to the New York City Health and Hospitals Corporation (HHC). It is important to bear in mind that privatization has more than one meaning, and that these meanings are not always consistent. Some argue that government should neither be the direct provider of nor pay for some activities in which it now engages. Examples sometimes used include municipal broadcasting facilities and parking garages. In these cases, privatization means that the public sector plays no role other than regulation; instead, the production and distribution of the good or service is dependent on private purchases and private firms. Such forms

1

of privatization may involve the sale of public assets to private firms, a transaction that additionally yields one-time revenues that are attractive to public officials seeking to balance their budgets.

Another form of privatization acknowledges a need for public payment to support a service, but argues that private firms can deliver the service more efficiently than a public agency can. In these cases, privatization takes the form of the government contracting with private firms. A long-standing example is the use of private construction firms to build public facilities, while a newer application is the use by some states of private firms to operate prisons.

Yet another version of privatization emphasizes the application of competition and market mechanisms in the production of public services. Advocates argue that competitive procedures, notably bidding, can achieve efficient results even when eligible organizations include nonprofit organizations and government agencies as well as for-profit firms. Examples include competitive bidding for home care services, employment placement services, and household refuse collection.

Each approach to privatization may be appropriate in certain circumstances—yet none may be desirable in other circumstances. This paper raises questions as to whether providing medical care is an appropriate role for local government and, if it is, which mechanisms might be most effective in achieving this purpose. The basic assumption of this paper is that ideology alone does not provide answers. The appropriate use of "privatization," however defined, is dependent on an understanding of the specific purpose society seeks to fulfill and the specific market conditions that exist or can be created. Thus, in considering whether and how to privatize the Health and Hospitals Corporation, it is necessary to understand its mission and the characteristics of the medical care marketplace in which it currently operates and will be operating in the future.

Medical care in New York City is one example of a marketplace whose workings can be understood fully only in a historical context. Accordingly, an important element of this paper traces the evolution of HHC's role in the local health care industry. Chapter 5, the last chapter of this paper, is intended as a reference for those readers deeply concerned with health care and is also a source of supporting evidence for some of the points made in the more explicitly policy-oriented sections of the paper. That chapter describes the circumstances behind the adoption of key policies that now shape HHC's operation, including its heavy reliance on contracts with private teaching institutions (known as "affiliation contracts") to secure medical staff, which dates from the early 1960s; the creation in 1970 of HHC as a public benefit corporation to operate municipal hospitals under a board of directors appointed by the mayor; the absence of clear rules for setting the size of the city's fiscal support for HHC, which has led to frequent midyear budget disruptions since the fiscal crises of the 1970s; and the more recent state-level emphasis on managed care, which has led HHC to organize and expand its own managed care plan.

Chapter 2 begins the policy analysis with a profile of the role HHC currently plays in the local marketplace. HHC's facilities include eleven acute care hospitals, five long-term care hospitals, and six freestanding diagnostic & treatment centers providing ambulatory care. (Since 1994, these facilities have been organized into six regional networks.) HHC's facilities account for about 23 percent of acute inpatient care in the city, over one-third of emergency room visits, and 37 percent of outpatient department visits. But HHC's market share is concentrated among the indigent. It provides nearly 40 percent of all inpatient care for those enrolled in Medicaid and a similar proportion for the poor lacking any insurance. HHC's ambulatory services to the indigent are an even larger share, leading it to be viewed by many as a family doctor to the poor. Moreover, many of the indigent relying on HHC for care have problems—such as drug and alcohol abuse, psychiatric disorders, and AIDS—that make them unattractive to private providers.

Chapter 3 examines the likely shape of the future medical care marketplace and analyzes how it might affect the future of HHC. First, the physician labor market is moving toward a condition of surplus supply, especially in surgical and some other specialties. This means HHC may no longer be obliged to rely so heavily on affiliations with private institutions to secure its physicians.

Second, medical care delivery is being reorganized into managed care plans staffed by designated groups of doctors and financed with periodic, fixed "capitation" payments based on enrollment, a marked contrast to the "freedom of choice" granted by traditional health insurance that reimbursed patients on a fee-for-service basis. While it is becoming widespread for all New Yorkers, managed care is especially relevant to those enrolled in Medicaid; current state plans are to require all nonelderly Medicaid eligibles to enroll in managed care plans within two years. This implies that HHC, whose major source of patients and revenues is Medicaid, must improve its capacity to operate as a managed care organization.

Third, the system for financing care of the indigent is changing in ways that are hard to predict. In the wake of President Clinton's unsuccessful effort to promote federal support of universal coverage, new federal funding seems unlikely, and congressionally initiated cuts are possible. New York State's Medicaid policies strongly favor capitation payments for this group, and state policies also have provided funds for the otherwise uninsured. This has permitted HHC to reduce its reliance on local tax funds; in fiscal year 1994, the direct appropriation from the city represented under 10 percent of HHC's revenues compared to 24 percent in 1985, and 36 percent in 1980. In contrast, state-controlled revenues including Medicaid and subsidies for the uninsured represented about two-thirds of HHC's revenues in 1994. This implies that state financing policies, as well as HHC's fiscal ties to the city, are crucial to the organization's future.

Chapter 4 considers two sets of policy options for HHC: specifically, the proposals recently set forth by Mayor Rudolph Giuliani and a set of recommendations prepared by the authors and endorsed by the Citizens Budget Commission. The mayor's proposals were announced in February 1995 and consist of (a) selling three acute care facilities—Coney Island Hospital, Elmhurst Hospital Center, and Queens Hospital Center; (b) appointing a small blue-ribbon commission to present a long-term plan for HHC. An initial critique of the mayor's proposals is its "sell now, plan later" approach; without a long-term vision of the future of HHC, there is no coherent basis for selecting any hospital or set of hospitals for sale or closure. Any rush to sell these facilities could endanger the viability of a plan for the future of HHC. Alternatively, if the mayor's yet unstated eventual goal is to eliminate HHC, then its wisdom should be questioned, for this would be a serious threat to access to medical care for many poor New Yorkers.

The recommended approach has three basic elements:

1. *There should continue to be a publicly accountable organization responsible for helping to ensure that New Yorkers gain access to needed medical care regardless of their ability to pay.* Absent significant national reforms that improve federal funding for the currently uninsured and promote access to private providers for all the indigent, there will remain a critical role for state and local government in

ensuring that poorer residents receive needed care. A public organization is needed to promote the mission currently assigned to HHC.

2. *The public entity given responsibility for this mission should be organized and operated in ways that differ significantly from the structure and processes now established for HHC.* The organization's governing board should be smaller and include appointees reflecting the interests of the state as well as the city. The organization should develop a financial relationship with the state that provides revenues primarily on a capitation basis and a fiscal relationship with the city that links revenues to specific services performed. Perhaps most important, the organization should operate primarily as a managed care plan with identified enrollees and financial incentives to reduce unnecessary utilization and shrink its inpatient bed capacity.

3. *The restructured public entity should make use of concepts of privatization to promote efficiency in its operations.* Opportunities to engage in forms of privatization include the sale of facilities with redundant beds, the development of productivity-based compensation arrangements with physicians to replace or supplement existing affiliation contracts, competitive bidding for support services such as laundry and meals, and competitive bidding for prison health services.

2.

Profile of the New York City Health and Hospitals Corporation

In considering the future of the New York City Health and Hospitals Corporation (HHC), it is important to have a clear picture of the roles it performs in the current health care market. What does HHC do? The most direct way to answer this question is to describe HHC's facilities and services.[1] However, this is only the first step in understanding the citywide role of HHC. A more complete understanding requires viewing HHC's services in the context of the New York City health care system.

HHC Facilities and Services

The HHC operates eleven acute care hospitals, five long-term care institutions, six diagnostic and treatment centers (D&T centers), and one HMO (Metroplus), as well as the city's Emergency Medical Service (EMS). In addition, each of the acute care hospitals (and one long-term care facility) operates an extensive ambulatory care program in its outpatient departments and emergency room. Most of the acute care hospitals also serve as a referral center for a network of smaller, ambulatory care facilities located in surrounding neighborhoods. HHC and the Department of Health have been working to develop and expand twenty of these centers through the Communi-Care initiative, launched by Mayor David Dinkins in 1993.

Under Mayor Giuliani, HHC's facilities have been reorganized into six regional networks; these networks are intended to promote vertical integration of ambulatory services, acute inpatient care, and skilled nursing care at long-term care facilities (see Table 2.1, pages 10–11). Five of the six networks have two acute care hospitals; the North Manhattan network has one acute facility—Harlem Hospital. All of the networks except the Queens network, which has a new Communi-Care center, contain at least one D&T center. The South Manhattan/North Brooklyn network is the largest and includes two long term-care facilities and two D&T centers in addition to two acute care facilities (Bellevue Hospital Center and Woodhull Medical and Mental Health Center).

The acute care hospitals operate a total of 8,091 beds, including 5,933 beds classified as general care, and range in size from 1,272 to 433 beds. The remaining beds are divided among mental health services (1,461 beds), rehabilitation (360 beds), tuberculosis (82 beds), and alcohol and drug treatment (255 beds). Occupancy rates for the acute care facilities in fiscal year 1994 averaged 79 percent, ranging from 72 percent at Harlem Hospital Center to 88 percent at Metropolitan Hospital Center.

The five long-term care facilities have 2,805 beds, most of which are at the two largest institutions: Coler Memorial Hospital has 775 skilled nursing care beds, 190 chronic care beds, and 60 rehabilitation beds, and Goldwater Memorial Hospital has 540 skilled nursing care beds, 322 chronic care beds, and 120 rehabilitation and related beds. Sea View, the only HHC facility on Staten Island, is a smaller nursing facility with 304 beds. Gouverneur, the smallest HHC facility with 210 skilled nursing care beds, also houses an extensive ambulatory care program through its D&T center. Neponsit is a 284-bed residential health care facility that provides less intensive long-term care in beds characterized as intermediate care. Occupancy rates for the long-term care facilities averaged 97 percent, ranging from 94 percent at Goldwater to 99 percent at Gouverneur.

The ambulatory care facilities operated by HHC are extensive. Fully 5.7 million ambulatory care visits were provided at HHC facilities in fiscal year 1994. Of this total, about 4.2 million, or 73 percent, were provided in conventional hospital outpatient departments; another 996,466, or almost 18 percent, were provided in emergency rooms; and the remaining 524,759, or 9 percent, were provided at health centers operated separately from the hospital facility. In a 1988 study, HHC estimated that about 34 percent of its ambulatory care visits are for primary care treatment (such as routine pediatric and maternity visits as well as less complex adult treatment); approximately 22 percent are for mental health services, including drug treatment, and another 22 percent are for more specialized medical care services.[2] The remaining visits are to emergency rooms and are believed to include a substantial volume of primary care services. Only a small fraction of emergency room visits represent serious trauma or truly emergency conditions.

Most HHC services are provided to poor New Yorkers. Although detailed data on the incomes of patients are not available, information relating to the source of payment supports this generalization (see Table 2.2, pages 12–13). In 1994, over three-quarters (76 percent) of HHC's inpatient days either were paid by Medicaid (63 percent) or were "self-pay" (13 percent), meaning they were not covered by any insurance. The self-pay category has a different meaning for the municipal and private hospitals. For HHC facilities, "self-pay" patients are almost exclusively uninsured poor, while at private facilities this group includes both uninsured poor and more affluent patients who actually pay directly for their care. Another 20 percent were paid by Medicare, the federal program covering the aged, and many of these patients are likely to have been poor elderly. Thus, fully 96 percent of HHC's inpatient care probably is provided to the indigent.

HHC's ambulatory services also reach primarily the indigent (see Table 2.3, page14). Among its hospital outpatient department visits, 39 percent are for Medicaid enrollees and 49 percent are for uninsured individuals who pay nothing or pay only a partial fee. Another 12 percent are for Medicare eligibles, and only a minute fraction are for privately insured patients. Among voluntary hospitals, outpatient department visits also are concentrated among the poor, but a far larger share (62 percent) are covered by Medicaid, while a much smaller share (16 percent) are uninsured.

A similar pattern is evident among emergency room visits. HHC's emergency room visits are primarily by Medicaid enrollees (37 percent) and the uninsured (48 percent). Voluntary hospital emergency rooms also serve a large share of Medicaid eligibles (32 percent), but proportionately fewer uninsured (30 percent).

HHC also operates Metroplus, an HMO open to Medicaid recipients and HHC employees. Metroplus had an enrollment of over

TABLE 2.1
SELECTED CHARACTERISTICS OF HHC FACILITIES, FISCAL YEAR 1994

NETWORK	BED COMPLEMENT					OCCUPANCY RATE	AMBUALTORY CARE VISITS	
	TOTAL	GENERAL CARE	PSYCHIATRY	LONG TERM	OTHER		EMERGENCY ROOM	OUTPATIENT CLINICS
South Bronx/North Manhattan–subtotal	2,301	1,006	231	965	99	N/A	179,631	748,667
Segundo Ruiz Belvis D&TC[a]	N/A	N/A	N/A	N/A	N/A	N/A	N/A	82,063
Coler Memorial Hospital[b]	1,025	0	0	965[d]	60	97.9%	N/A	N/A
Lincoln Medical and Mental Health Center[c]	669	614	55	N/A	0	83.9%	114,442	380,333
Metropolitan Hospital Center[c]	607	392	176	N/A	39	87.8%	65,189	286,271
North Bronx–subtotal	1,256	947	172	0	137	N/A	172,642	655,934
Bronx Municipal Hospital Center[c]	823	586	125	N/A	112	75.8%	99,604	325,854
Morrisania D&TC[a]	N/A	N/A	N/A	N/A	N/A	N/A	N/A	140,590
North Central Bronx Hospital[c]	433	361	47	N/A	25	75.8%	73,038	189,490
Queens–subtotal	1,486	813	224	284	165	N/A	182,777	656,693
Elmhurst Hospital Center[c]	646	428	158	N/A	60	83.2%	117,713	397,885
Neponsit Health Care Center[a]	284	N/A	N/A	284	0	99.0%	N/A	N/A
Queens Hospital Center[c]	556	385	66	N/A	105	73.9%	65,064	258,808
Brooklyn/Staten Island–subtotal	2,048	1,285	296	304	163	N/A	233,546	949,230
Coney Island Hospital[c]	490	427	30	N/A	33	87.3%	74,378	336,112
East New York D&TC[a]	N/A	N/A	N/A	N/A	N/A	N/A	N/A	73,818

TABLE 2.1 (CONTINUED)
SELECTED CHARACTERISTICS OF HHC FACILITIES, FISCAL YEAR 1994

NETWORK	BED COMPLEMENT					OCCUPANCY RATE	AMBULATORY CARE VISITS	
	TOTAL	GENERAL CARE	PSYCHIATRY	LONG TERM	OTHER		EMERGENCY ROOM	OUTPATIENT CLINICS
Kings County Hospital Center[c]	1,254	858	266	N/A	130	73.0%	159,168	538,426
Sea View Hospital, Rehabilitation Center, and Home[b]	304	N/A	N/A	304	0	96.6%	N/A	874
North Manhattan–subtotal	740	623	66	0	51		64,692	576,295
Harlem Hospital Center[c]	740	623	66	N/A	51	72.4%	64,692	476,317
Renaissance/Sydenham NFCC[a]	N/A	N/A	N/A	N/A	N/A	N/A	N/A	99,978
South Manhattan/North Brooklyn–subtotal	3,065	1,259	472	1,072	262		163,178	1,120,891
Bellevue Hospital Center[c]	1,272	851	339	N/A	82	76.1%	83,223	461,636
Cumberland D&TC[a]	N/A	N/A	N/A	N/A	N/A	N/A	N/A	128,310
Goldwater Memorial Hospital[b]	982	0	0	862[d]	120	94.0%	N/A	N/A
Gouverneur Nursing Facility and D&TC[ab]	210	N/A	N/A	210	0	99.4%	N/A	316,034
Woodhull Medical and Mental Health Center[c]	601	408	133	N/A	60	84.0%	79,955	214,911
Total	10,896	5,933	1,461	2,625	877	83.1%	996,466	4,707,710

Source: United Hospital Fund, *The State of New York City's Municipal Hospital System*, New York, fiscal year 1994 edition.

[a] Diagnostic & Treatment Center (D&TC); [b] Long-Term Care Facility; [c] Acute Care Facility; [d] Includes 190 and 322 chronic care beds at Coler and Goldwater, respectively.

N/A = Not applicable.

TABLE 2.2
PATIENT DAYS BY PAYER AND HOSPITAL
NEW YORK CITY, 1991 AND 1992 THIRD QUARTERS AND 1994 SECOND QUARTER

	TOTAL		MEDICARE		MEDICAID		BLUE CROSS		COMMERCIAL		OTHER[a]	
	NUMBER	%	NUMBER	%	NUMBER	%	NUMBER	%	NUMBER	%	NUMBER	%
1991												
All Hospitals	2,698,412	100.0	1,007,775	37.3	875,090	32.4	397,064	14.7	135,421	5.0	283,062	10.5
HHC	568,161	100.0	114,536	20.0	316,956	55.8	25,862	4.5	6,408	1.1	104,399	18.4
Voluntary	2,003,402	100.0	823,584	41.1	537,124	26.8	349,252	17.4	123,098	6.2	170,344	8.5
Proprietary	99,193	100.0	62,015	62.5	12,509	12.6	16,103	16.2	4,061	4.1	4,505	4.5
State	27,656	100.0	7,640	27.6	8,501	30.7	5,847	21.1	1,854	6.7	3,814	13.8
1992												
All Hospitals	2,689,544	100.0	987,791	36.7	937,108	34.9	349,186	13.0	125,536	4.7	289,923	10.8
HHC	607,785	100.0	116,693	19.2	357,245	58.8	22,489	3.7	8,016	1.3	103,342	17.0
Voluntary	1,956,156	100.0	801,159	41.0	556,775	28.5	309,367	15.8	111,707	5.7	177,148	9.1
Proprietary	97,744	100.0	61,996	63.4	14,346	14.7	11,871	12.1	4,278	4.4	5,253	5.4
State	27,859	100.0	7,943	28.5	8,742	31.4	5,459	19.6	1,535	5.5	4,180	15.0

TABLE 2.2 (CONTINUED)
PATIENT DAYS BY PAYER AND HOSPITAL
NEW YORK CITY, 1991 AND 1992 THIRD QUARTERS AND 1994 SECOND QUARTER

	TOTAL		MEDICARE		MEDICAID		BLUE CROSS		COMMERCIAL		OTHER[a]	
	NUMBER	%	NUMBER	%	NUMBER	%	NUMBER	%	NUMBER	%	NUMBER	%
1994												
All Hospitals	2,574,082	100.0	961,360	37.3	961,218	37.3	259,186	10.1	169,719	6.6	222,599	8.6
HHC	594,336	100.0	117,090	19.7	376,447	63.3	16,323	2.7	7,128	1.2	77,348	13.0
Voluntary	1,555,661	100.0	664,646	42.7	448,443	28.8	198,251	12.7	126,082	8.1	118,239	7.6
Proprietary	397,436	100.0	171,253	43.1	127,539	32.1	40,210	10.1	35,653	9.0	22,781	5.7
State	26,649	100.0	8,371	31.4	8,789	33.0	4,402	16.5	856	3.2	4,231	15.9

Source: Compiled from data obtained from United Hospital Fund of New York.

[a] Includes self-pay and all payers not listed elsewhere.

TABLE 2.3
AMBULATORY CARE VISITS BY PAYER,
HHC AND VOLUNTARY HOSPITALS, 1992[a]

| | VOLUNTARY HOSPITALS | | | | HHC | | | |
| | OUTPATIENT VISITS | | EMERGENCY ROOM VISITS | | OUTPATIENT VISITS | | EMERGENCY ROOM VISITS | |
	NUMBER	% OF TOTAL	NUMBER	% OF TOTAL	NUMBER	% OF TOTAL	NUMBER	% OF TOTAL
Medicaid	3,084,060	61.8	589,068	31.9	1,200,618	39.4	383,945	37.2
Medicare	653,741	13.1	212,367	11.5	350,434	11.5	114,564	11.1
Blue Cross	14,971	0.3	227,139	12.3	3,047	0.1	36,124	3.5
Uninsured/ Self-Pay	813,433	16.3	552,153	29.9	1,493,155	49.0	497,477	48.2
Commercial	424,183	8.5	265,920	14.4	914	0.0	310	0.0
Total	4,990,388	100.0	1,846,647	100.0	3,048,168	100.0	1,032,402	100.0

Sources: Voluntary hospital data from United Hospital Fund of New York. Health and Hospitals Corportion data from HHC Blue Cross supplements to the institutional cost reports.

a 1992 calendar year data for voluntary hospitals and 1992 fiscal year data for municipal hospitals.

36,000 Medicaid clients in April 1995. It was the third-largest managed care plan serving Medicaid eligibles and accounted for about 10 percent of all Medicaid managed care enrollment in New York City (see Table 2.4, pages 16–17).

Finally, it should be noted that HHC oversees the Emergency Medical Service (EMS), which operates municipal ambulances and coordinates activities with ambulances operated by voluntary hospitals and other organizations. The EMS provided nearly 1.3 million ambulance responses in fiscal year 1994.[3] In his executive budget for fiscal year 1996, Mayor Giuliani proposed transferring the EMS to the Fire Department.

CITYWIDE ROLES

Clearly, the HHC is a large system that provides a substantial volume of care to the poor. But from a citywide perspective, how significant are HHC services? The municipal hospitals represent nearly 19 percent of all hospital beds in the city, but does this nearly one-fifth of the system have any distinctive characteristics aside from its municipal auspices?

At least four distinctive roles have been claimed and deserve discussion. The first two relate to the poor. First, HHC often is described as the "family doctor" to the poor, providing them with routine ambulatory care that the middle class generally receives in private practitioners' offices. Second, the HHC is described as the major source of inpatient care for the poor; providing them with the more specialized services middle-class patients receive in voluntary hospitals.

A third distinctive mission of the municipal system is said to be its willingness and ability to care for groups with special problems beyond lack of money or insurance—notably substance abusers and the mentally ill—who are often unwelcome at private facilities. Finally, the HHC is described as providing specialized services, such as trauma care, for the community at large; in this role, the HHC is thought to represent a unique source of service for all New Yorkers.

FAMILY DOCTOR TO THE POOR

The nearly 6 million ambulatory care visits provided by the HHC facilities include a large number of visits that represent routine care equivalent to that which many citizens receive at the offices of private

TABLE 2.4
NEW YORK CITY MEDICAID MANAGED CARE ENROLLMENT BY PLAN
1992, 1994, AND 1995

PLAN	1992 ENROLLMENT	1994 ENROLLMENT	1995 ENROLLMENT
Health Insurance Plan of Greater New York	48,845	79,221	79,948
Oxford Health Plan*	735	33,359	39,062
U.S. Healthcare Inc.*	1,410	30,143	31,837
Bronx Health Plan	13,349	29,260	32,611
Managed Health Care of N.Y.*	N/A	28,297	35,112
Metroplus	4,584	26,972	36,433
Manhattan PHSP "CenterCare"	4,174	14,878	19,400
Catholic Health Services Plan	N/A	13,379	18,835
Lutheran Medical Center/Health Care Plus	5,656	10,350	10,905
Health First	N/A	9,743	27,496
Prime Care New York	160	5,409	5,367
Healthnet	184	2,843	2,800
Managed Health Inc.*	N/A	2,672	2,890
Cigna Healthcare of N.Y.*	242	2,523	2,478

TABLE 2.4 (CONTINUED)
NEW YORK CITY MEDICAID MANAGED CARE ENROLLMENT BY PLAN
1992, 1994, AND 1995

PLAN	1992 ENROLLMENT	1994 ENROLLMENT	1995 ENROLLMENT
Aetna Health Plans*	444	1,446	1,432
Staten Island Hospital	N/A	376	614
Prime Care Queens	N/A	304	1,230
Beth Abraham CCM	N/A	253	286
Elderplan Inc.	124	128	134
Metlife*	N/A	N/A	23
New York Health Plan*	N/A	N/A	4,729
Total	79,907	291,556	353,622

Sources: 1992 data from City of New York, Office of Medicaid Managed Care, New York City Medicaid Managed Care Plan, November 1992. 1994 data (as of December 1, 1994) and 1995 data (as of April 1, 1995) provided by New York City Health and Hospitals Corporation, Department of Planning Services.
N/A = Not applicable; plan was either not enrolling Medicaid recipients or did not exist in 1992.

*Denotes a commercial or for-profit plan.

practitioners. This includes the approximately one out of every five ambulatory care visits characterized earlier as primary care as well as a substantial proportion of the nearly 1 million emergency room visits. Given the large volume of primary care at municipal facilities, it is likely that a large majority of the poor—both Medicaid eligible and uninsured—receive at least a portion of their routine medical care from HHC.

But in considering the "family doctor" claim, it is important to know that the poor utilize other sources of primary care. Private practitioners in the fee-for-service system have been reluctant to provide care to those enrolled in Medicaid due to low fee scales ($11 for a physician office visit) established under the state Medicaid program. Those physicians who did treat Medicaid patients often did so at shared facilities known as "Medicaid mills," which relied on a high volume of routine services to generate enough revenue to retain the physicians. Recent initiatives to promote managed care seek to provide Medicaid patients with improved access to high-quality primary care physicians by improving the financial incentives of caring for Medicaid patients. Doctors who join a commercial Medicaid managed care plan typically receive a portion of the periodic capitation payment (or fixed payment per person enrolled) as a form of salary. As of April 1995, about 120,000 Medicaid beneficiaries were enrolled in a commercially sponsored managed care plan providing access to a private physician for ambulatory care (see Table 2.4).

In addition, as Table 2.3 shows, voluntary hospitals' emergency rooms and outpatient departments provide a significant amount of care to the poor. Among those with Medicaid coverage, voluntary hospitals provided more hospital-based care than HHC. In 1992, voluntary hospitals provided nearly 3.1 million Medicaid outpatient clinic visits, as well as 589,068 Medicaid emergency room visits; the comparable numbers for HHC are 1.2 million Medicaid outpatient visits and 383,945 Medicaid emergency room visits. (It should be noted that HHC provided an additional 160,423 Medicaid visits at its D&T centers.)

The municipal role is larger, however, for those lacking third-party coverage, although the voluntary hospitals still play a significant role. Among the uninsured, voluntary hospitals provided 813,433 outpatient clinic visits and 552,153 emergency room visits, compared to HHC's 1,493,155 uninsured outpatient visits and 497,477 uninsured emergency room visits. In addition, HHC provided 164,153 uninsured visits at its D&T centers.

Nevertheless, given the substantial volume of ambulatory care provided to the indigent at voluntary hospitals and by the growing number of private practitioners through commercial managed care plans, it is likely that the HHC accounts for a minority of all primary care visits by the poor. Among Medicaid enrollees, a significant majority of the care is provided by voluntary hospitals and, in rapidly increasing numbers, by physicians engaged by commercial HMOs. Among the uninsured poor, one of two utilization patterns is likely to be followed: One group uses municipal facilities for some of its care, but receives most of its care at other sources. (For example, a child with a serious chronic or congenital condition is treated for that condition at the specialized clinic of a voluntary hospital but is treated for a routine respiratory infection at a municipal emergency room.) A second group relies almost exclusively on a municipal facility for routine ambulatory services and more serious acute care.

The factors that determine whether and how poor, uninsured New Yorkers and Medicaid beneficiaries use municipal facilities reflect complex "push" and "pull" factors. These factors also influence whether a Medicaid recipient chooses HHC's Metroplus over another managed care plan.

Looking at the "pull" factors, the facilities' attractiveness depends on the convenience of their location, the way in which services are organized, the skill and courtesy of the staff, and the condition of the physical plant. In recent years, the HHC has reorganized and modernized some of its ambulatory care facilities; it is likely that these improvements have led some residents to select a municipal facility or Metroplus as their "first choice" source of care.

The "push" factors represent the nature of the alternatives. If other facilities are not conveniently located or a nearby voluntary hospital displays an unwillingness to treat routine conditions that do not meet the teaching needs of the staff, then patients necessarily make use of municipal facilities. In addition, some voluntary hospitals limit the volume of Medicaid or uncompensated care they provide, primarily because they are not reimbursed fully for this care through the state's Medicaid and uncompensated care programs. In such circumstances, patients may be pushed into using a municipal facility by subtle (or not so subtle) practices of a voluntary facility.

INPATIENT CARE FOR THE POOR

Patterns of utilization for inpatient care vary from those for ambulatory care. Just as middle-class citizens may seek or be referred to a specialist rather than their "family doctor" to treat more difficult conditions, poorer New Yorkers may seek inpatient care at sources other than their site of primary care. To what extent does HHC provide inpatient care to the indigent? In 1994, the inpatient days at HHC facilities represented 23 percent of the citywide total (see Table 2.2). But HHC patients are disproportionately poor; municipal facilities accounted for over 39 percent of Medicaid inpatient days, and nearly 35 percent of all uninsured or self-pay days.

The HHC undeniably is a major source of inpatient care for the poor, providing inpatient services to many patients for whom it is also a source of ambulatory care. But HHC's citywide role in inpatient care is smaller than in ambulatory care. Municipal facilities account for about 23 percent of inpatient days, compared to over one-third of emergency room visits and over 37 percent of all outpatient department visits. This suggests that some patients who rely on HHC for routine ambulatory care obtain their more specialized inpatient care at private facilities. In part, this is attributable to a greater willingness of private facilities to provide inpatient rather than ambulatory care to the indigent, a situation that reflects the more generous payment for inpatient services by Medicaid, the concern of voluntary hospital administrators and physicians with maintaining high occupancy rates in the face of declining aggregate demand for inpatient care, and the fact that the inpatient care represents treatment of more serious conditions better suited to specialty teaching programs than most outpatient care.

Although the subject has not been studied systematically, the indigent patients who are admitted to private facilities probably are not randomly selected from among the poor. Those with Medicaid coverage are more likely to be admitted than those who are uninsured; those with conditions of interest to teaching faculty at academic medical centers also may enjoy better access; and finally, those with psychiatric or social problems are less likely to be admitted because they are harder to treat while in the hospital and harder to place when treatment is completed.

CARE FOR SPECIAL GROUPS OF PATIENTS

As the foregoing discussion suggests, access to medical care is not simply a matter of money. Some of the indigent, even those with Medicaid coverage, suffer special access problems because their psychological or other disorders result in discrimination by medical practitioners. The principal examples are treatment for drug abuse, alcoholism, certain types of psychiatric disorders, AIDS, and treatment of most medical conditions for homeless individuals.

The HHC has assumed a major role in caring for these patients. It operates 255 beds for alcoholism and drug treatment, and a notable portion of its regular medical and surgical beds probably are filled with patients suffering some substance addiction as well as other acute medical conditions. As patients with psychiatric problems were kept out of state mental health institutions in the late 1980s, the HHC expanded its psychiatric facilities to reach 1,672 beds in 1989, accounting for fully 49 percent of all psychiatric beds in the city (see Table 2.5, pages 22–23). Although the psychiatric bed total has since been reduced to 1,461, HHC still accounts for 45 percent of all psychiatric beds citywide. The HHC's annual outpatient department workload includes approximately 794,000 drug treatment visits (primarily in Methadone-maintenance clinics) and 506,000 psychiatric visits.[4]

Another indicator of HHC's services to the difficult-to-serve is the large number of "alternative level of care" (ALOC) days it provides for patients who do not need acute inpatient services but who remain in the hospital only because alternative care arrangements, such as home care or nursing home care, are not available. In 1994, ALOC days at HHC accounted for 4.7 percent of total days, compared to a citywide average of 2.9 percent.[5] A disproportionate share of HHC alternative level of care days are for patients with very long stays indicating severe problems in finding a new home. These patients include "boarder babies" who remain in hospitals after treatment for abuse or neglect pending placement in a foster home, as well as the homeless mentally ill.

The HHC also plays a disproportionately large role in caring for AIDS patients. HHC provides one-third of all inpatient and 58 percent of all outpatient care to the city's AIDS patients. In fiscal year 1994, HHC facilities had over seven hundred AIDS patients on average daily;

TABLE 2.5
GENERAL CARE HOSPITAL BEDS IN NEW YORK CITY
1980–1993

ALL HOSPITALS

YEAR	TOTAL[a] GENERAL CARE	MEDICAL/ SURGICAL	PEDIATRICS	OBSTETRICS	PSYCHIATRIC CARE
1980	33,596	28,723	2,855	2,018	2,812
1981	32,778	27,945	2,847	1,986	3,006
1982	32,656	27,863	2,879	1,914	3,074
1983	32,708	28,086	2,740	1,882	3,110
1984	32,111	27,522	2,707	1,882	3,179
1985	32,026	27,446	2,776	1,804	3,243
1986	31,251	26,776	2,670	1,805	3,305
1987	30,263	25,807	2,659	1,797	3,563
1988	29,427	24,980	2,650	1,797	3,691
1989	29,610	25,070	2,654	1,886	3,411
1990	29,673	25,077	2,717	1,879	2,906
1991	29,870	25,271	2,722	1,877	3,230
1992	29,517	24,844	2,811	1,862	3,235
1993	28,866	24,423	2,612	1,831	3,328

PERCENTAGE
 CHANGE

1980–86	-7.0	-6.8	-6.5	-10.6	17.5
1986–88	-5.8	-6.7	-0.7	-0.4	11.7
1988–93	-1.9	-2.2	-1.4	1.9	-9.8
1980–93	-14.1	-15.0	-8.5	-9.3	18.3

TABLE 2.5 (CONTINUED)
GENERAL CARE HOSPITAL BEDS IN NEW YORK CITY
1980–1993

MUNICIPAL HOSPITALS

YEAR	TOTAL[a] GENERAL CARE	MEDICAL/ SURGICAL	PEDIATRICS	OBSTETRICS	PSYCHIATRIC CARE
1980	6,629	5,279	838	512	1,367
1981	6,072	4,753	820	499	1,353
1982	6,078	4,753	826	499	1,368
1983	5,954	4,667	800	487	1,368
1984	5,770	4,515	761	494	1,401
1985	5,856	4,569	787	500	1,436
1986	5,871	4,578	793	500	1,565
1987	5,632	4,339	793	500	1,580
1988	5,241	3,948	793	500	1,635
1989	5,243	3,916	827	500	1,672
1990	5,471	4,091	864	516	1,438
1991	5,463	4,084	863	516	1,477
1992	5,476	4,097	863	516	1,461
1993	5,356	4,104	736	516	1,461

PERCENTAGE CHANGE

1980–86	-11.4	-13.3	-5.4	-2.3	14.5
1986–88	-10.7	-13.8	0.0	0.0	4.5
1988–93	2.2	4.0	-7.2	3.2	-10.6
1980–93	-19.2	-22.3	-12.2	0.8	6.9

Sources: Kenneth Thorpe, "Health Care," in *Setting Municipal Priorities, 1990,* ed. Charles Brecher and Raymond D. Horton (New York: New York University Press, 1989), updated with United Hospital Fund of New York data. Figures for 1980 and 1981 are for January 1 of that year; figures for 1982–89 are for December 31 of the preceding year.

a General Care total excludes psychiatric beds.

fully one in ten of HHC's general care beds was occupied by an AIDS patient. Similarly, with 301 tuberculosis cases, HHC treated fully 46 percent of the city's inpatient tuberculosis patients.[6]

The absence of a clear definition and appropriate data make it difficult to estimate precisely what share of HHC's workload is accounted for by special patient groups, and the figure undoubtedly varies by facility and service. However, a significant minority of all services in the city is accounted for by these patients, and citywide, the HHC may provide the majority of their care.

SPECIALIZED, COMMUNITY-WIDE SERVICES

In addition to caring for the poor, local public hospitals often serve as community-wide resources for specialized facilities used by the middle class. Nationwide, local public hospitals often are a community's sole source for certain types of burn and other trauma care and for other specialized services such as care for very premature newborns.

In New York City, the major community-wide service of the HHC is trauma care. Municipal emergency rooms are an important resource for all citizens, especially for members of the city's uniformed services who are injured while on duty. While voluntary hospitals provide emergency care for a majority of insured New Yorkers, HHC proves to be the more accessible resource for some middle-class citizens in distress. In 1992, about 36,000 people with Blue Cross coverage used an HHC emergency room; this represented about one of every seven emergency room visits by those with Blue Cross coverage (see Table 2.3).

Aside from emergency room capacity, the HHC has few community-wide services to benefit affluent and poor New Yorkers alike. Large, voluntary academic medical centers have most of the specialized equipment and services in the New York City health care industry. The HHC generally has relied on affiliated private institutions to provide specialized services to patients initially admitted to a municipal hospital. The most notable and well publicized exception to this pattern is the microsurgery team at Bellevue Hospital, which treats victims of accidents who require specialized skills for restoring severed limbs.

3.

FORCES SHAPING THE NEW YORK CITY HEALTH AND HOSPITALS CORPORATION'S FUTURE

The health care industry is widely regarded as one of the most dynamic sectors of the U.S. economy. New York City is not immune from the forces reshaping the industry nationwide, and these elements of change should be considered when designing the future of the New York City Health and Hospitals Corporation (HHC). Three forces in particular should be examined for their implications for the future structure of HHC: the changing physician labor market, the reorganization of health care delivery into managed care plans, and the uncertain financial arrangements for care for the indigent and uninsured.

THE PHYSICIAN LABOR MARKET

For much of this century, the United States was characterized as having a physician shortage. Efforts begun early in the 1900s to improve the quality of medical education led to a relatively small number of accredited medical schools. Political pressures from the American Medical Association to keep competition among physicians limited added to the tight control kept on medical school places. In 1965, the United States had 84 accredited medical schools graduating 7,409 physicians; the ratio of physicians to population was 124 per 100,000, which had not grown for decades. (By contrast, in 1993, there were 126 accredited medical schools graduating 15,466 physicians, with the ratio of physicians to 100,000 population at 204.)[1]

It was in the context of this very tight physician labor market that Mayor Robert Wagner and the city's hospital commissioner, Dr. Ray Trussell, implemented the teaching affiliation policy for municipal hospitals during the early 1960s. The scarcity of physicians and their inclination to follow middle-class patients to the suburbs meant public hospitals could no longer rely on voluntary efforts of community physicians to staff the hospital wards and clinics. Nor was it practical to try to hire physicians as salaried civil servants. The then-appropriate answer was to affiliate with teaching institutions; in exchange for some public funding and the availability of patients for residents' training and faculty clinical research, the teaching institution took responsibility for staffing the municipal hospitals.

This bargain, negotiated on a hospital-by-hospital basis, solved a crisis situation in the early 1960s and has provided some enduring benefits for the municipal system. The affiliated hospitals generally are able to hire a sufficient number of physicians to provide most of the services their clients need.

However, in reviewing the merits of the affiliation strategy, three points that qualify its success should be kept in mind. First, the policy has not been uniformly implemented at all HHC facilities; its benefits therefore also vary among facilities. The freestanding ambulatory centers and one long-term care hospital have no affiliates and hire their staff directly; some acute care facilities have a mix of affiliate staff and directly employed personnel (who may or may not be supervised by affiliate faculty); and affiliated medical services vary in the extent to which residency programs are integrated between the two institutions. The corollary to these varying arrangements is a wide variation in the extent to which municipal hospitals face difficulty in attracting sufficient medical staff.

For example, in 1992, a blue-ribbon commission appointed by Mayor David Dinkins to investigate HHC (known as the Barondess Commission) found that: (1) at Bellevue Hospital all the residencies are integrated with the New York University Medical Center, 83 percent of the residents are graduates of U.S. medical schools (USMGs), and 80 percent of the house staff positions were filled through the national matching program (the latter two figures are commonly accepted indicators of the quality of house staff); (2) at Harlem Hospital, the residency programs generally are not integrated with those at Columbia University's private affiliate, Presbyterian Hospital, only 38 percent of the residents were USMGs, and 65 percent of the positions were filled by the national match; (3) at Woodhull Hospital, the affiliate is a private group of physicians who deliver most of the services, and, among the residents, only 16 percent are USMGs and most positions are filled outside the national match.[2] In brief, few generalizations can be made about the staffing benefits of affiliations because the arrangements vary significantly.

Second, the affiliation policy represents a significant cost for HHC. In fiscal year 1994, the affiliations accounted for $512 million, or about 14 percent of HHC's total expenses (see Table 3.1, pages 28–29). Moreover, the costs of the affiliation policy extend beyond the direct outlays for physicians. Most of the affiliations are with teaching institutions, and caring for patients in a teaching setting generates costs not incurred in other community hospitals. Teaching patients are usually given more diagnostic tests, sometimes receive more aggressive treatments, and typically have longer lengths of stay. These additional indirect costs are difficult to quantify accurately but undoubtedly are significant. Using a methodology based on the one used by the federal Medicare program to pay hospitals for these indirect costs yields, the HHC estimates it incurs between $200 and $250 million in indirect education costs.[3]

Third, there are conflicts between the teaching needs of the academic affiliates and the service needs of HHC patients. A primary objective of academic affiliates is to sustain specialized teaching programs by gaining access to numerous patients with a broad range of conditions, including a sufficient number of patients requiring specialized procedures to meet national certification requirements for graduate training programs. This specialty orientation sometimes conflicts with HHC's need to provide a large volume of routine care, especially in its outpatient facilities. Outpatient services staffed by affiliate physicians and residents are typically organized by specialty into numerous clinics, and waiting time may be greatest at clinics providing more routine services. HHC has difficulty reorganizing services and shifting the mix of specialty physicians at its facilities because the desired changes conflict with teaching affiliates' missions and goals. Alternatively, affiliates may withdraw services from HHC facilities if an adequate teaching volume is available at other sites, despite a remaining need for the services among HHC patients.

The already varied balance of costs and benefits associated with affiliation policies is likely to change even more due to long-term forces

TABLE 3.1

NEW YORK CITY HEALTH AND HOSPITALS CORPORATION REVENUES AND EXPENDITURES, SELECTED CITY FISCAL YEARS 1970–1994 (DOLLARS IN MILLIONS)

	1970		1980		1985		1989		1990		1992		1993		1994	
	$	% of Total	$	% of Total	$	% of Total	$	% of Total	$	% of Total	$	% of Total	$	% of Total	$	% of Total
REVENUES	475	100.0	1,260	100.0	1,946	100.0	2,582	100.0	2,782	100.0	3,068	100.0	3,149	100.0	3,492	100.0
Third-Party	252	53.1	772	61.3	1,446	74.3	1,907	73.9	2,243	80.6	2,719	88.6	2,761	87.7	3,083	88.3
Medicaid	252	53.1	431	34.2	931	47.8	1,129	43.7	1,335	48.0	1,596	52.0	1,714	54.4	1,900	54.4
Medicare[a]	NA	NA	216	17.1	238	12.2	389	15.1	406	14.6	371	12.1	391	12.4	447	12.8
Blue Cross	0	0.0	56	4.4	91	4.7	119	4.6	114	4.1	117	3.8	105	3.3	91	2.6
Bad debt/charity care pool	NAP	NAP	NAP	NAP	NAP	NAP	89	3.4	198	7.1	454	14.8	354	11.2	431	12.3
Other	0	0.0	69	5.5	186	9.6	181	7.0	190	6.8	181	5.9	197	6.3	214	6.1
New York City subsidy	219	46.1	447	35.5	465	23.9	626	24.2	481	17.3	288	9.4	319	10.1	343	9.8
Other	4	0.8	41	3.3	35	1.8	49	1.9	58	2.1	61	2.0	69	2.2	66	1.9
EXPENDITURES	475	100.0	1,238	100.0	2,019	100.0	2,646	100.0	2,890	100.0	3,242	100.0	3,443	100.0	3,639	100.0
Personal service (including fringes)	NA	NA	764	61.7	1,196	59.2	1,637	61.9	1,821	63.0	1,971	60.8	2,116	61.5	2,216	60.9
Other-than-personal service	NA	NA	222	17.9	398	19.7	481	18.2	490	17.0	617	19.0	614	17.8	653	17.9

TABLE 3.1 (CONTINUED)
NEW YORK CITY HEALTH AND HOSPITALS CORPORATION REVENUES AND EXPENDITURES, SELECTED CITY FISCAL YEARS 1970–1994 (DOLLARS IN MILLIONS)

	1970		1980		1985		1989		1990		1992		1993		1994	
	$	% OF TOTAL	$	% OF TOTAL	$	% OF TOTAL	$	% OF TOTAL	$	% OF TOTAL	$	% OF TOTAL	$	% OF TOTAL	$	% OF TOTAL
EXPENDITURES (continued)																
Affiliation																
contract expenses	NA	NA	176	14.2	273	13.5	348	13.2	395	13.7	431	13.3	472	13.7	512	14.1
Depreciation	NA	NA	45	3.6	100	5.0	105	4.0	116	4.0	141	4.3	144	4.2	155	4.3
Interest	NA	NA	31	2.5	52	2.6	75	2.8	68	2.4	82	2.5	97	2.8	103	2.8
SURPLUS/(DEFICIT)	0		22		(73)		(64)		(108)		(174)		(294)		(147)	

	1970	1980	1985	1989	1990	1992	1993	1994
Subsidy as a percentage of total revenues	46.1	35.5	23.9	24.2	17.3	9.4	10.1	9.8

Sources: Data for 1970 are from City of New York, *Expense Budget for 1969–70*, p. 443. Data for all other years are from the New York City Health and Hospitals Corporation, *Consolidated Financial Statements*, 1975 to 1994 editions. Data for 1992–94 are adjusted to reflect provision for bad debt as a subtraction from revenues rather than as added expenses to make these years comparable to earlier years. For 1993 and 1994, bad debt was allocated by third-party revenue source based on percentage distribution of bad debt in 1992.

[a] Medicare revenues in 1970 were not shown separately; they are included with Medicaid revenues.

NAP = Not applicable. NA = Not available.

at work in the physician labor market. The supply of physicians has become more abundant than was the case when affiliations were established, and this is likely to continue in the foreseeable future. From 1970 to 1992, the physician-to-population ratio grew nationally from 125 to 204 per 100,000; in New York City, the growth was from 261 to 352 physicians per 100,000 population. The city's physician-to-population ratio is already more than 50 percent above the national average and it continues to rise (see Table 3.2, pages 32–33).

The city's physician supply has three other distinguishing characteristics besides its relative abundance. First, it is heavily oriented to hospital-based practice. Nearly half the city's physicians are in hospital-based practices compared to about one-quarter nationally. This reflects the large concentration of teaching hospitals in the city, and their complement of full-time staff as well as salaried residents. Second, the city is well endowed with office-based specialists. For medical and other specialists, the local physician-to-population ratio is about 60 percent greater than the national average. Third, New York has a shortage of general and family practitioners. The local ratio of these physicians to population is 10 per 100,000, less than half the national rate of 23 per 100,000. Nationally, and to an even greater extent in New York City, people rely on specialists to serve as their source of primary care.

The shift toward specialists can be explained partly by their higher and faster-rising incomes (see Table 3.3, pages 34–35). In 1982, the national mean net income for radiologists ($136,800) was only slightly less than double that of general/family practice physicians ($71,900); by 1991, radiologists' mean income grew to $229,800, more than double the figure for general care physicians ($111,500). In the Middle Atlantic region, general care physicians' mean income ($100,000) was fully $71,000, or 42 percent, below the average of all physicians; obstetricians and anesthesiologists received the highest compensation in the region, $260,000 and $240,500 respectively.

In the foreseeable future, specialists are likely to remain relatively abundant, while primary care physicians remain in relatively short supply. Some recent public policy initiatives seek to alter the balance. The federal government has begun to increase payments under the Medicare program for primary care services in order to narrow the gap between specialist and general care physician incomes; medical schools also are initiating programs to encourage students to pursue primary care careers. Nonetheless, the likely prospect is that in many areas specialists will continue to supplement family practice physicians in meeting the primary care needs of patients.

These trends have two important implications for HHC's affiliation policies. First, with respect to recruiting specialists, HHC will have more flexibility and more bargaining leverage with its affiliates as a result of the growing supply. HHC need not rely exclusively on teaching institutions to recruit specialists, and may be able to obtain the services of academic-based physicians at more competitive prices. By contracting for a large volume of specific, specialized services at one or more of its regional networks (as opposed to individual hospitals), HHC may be able to obtain high-quality services at costs lower than those offered by current affiliates.

Second, affiliation contracts may not be the best way to meet the need for primary care physicians. The teaching institutions are not well positioned to recruit family practitioners and other primary care doctors; their strength lies in having specialists and specialized services. HHC may need to develop new mechanisms for employing primary care physicians, a challenge it began to address with significant salary increases for those it already employs directly.

However, for the long term, the ability to attract more physicians to primary care practice is likely to depend on the creation of new practice and payment arrangements for them. This, in turn, is linked to the changes in the structure of medical care that are increasingly evident both nationally and locally.

REORGANIZATION OF HEALTH CARE DELIVERY

The United States has long had a pluralistic medical care system, but two distinct modes of delivery were behind the diverse set of for-profit, voluntary, and public institutions. Most working Americans fit a pattern of relying on private physicians in office-based practice for their care; if hospitalization were required, the physician would make arrangements at a hospital at which he or she had admitting privileges. This care would be priced by the physicians on a fee-for-service basis and by the hospital on a per diem or per admission basis. The costs would be the patients' responsibility, but insurance purchased at the workplace would cover the hospital bill and significant reimbursement would be available for physicians' services from private insurance companies. The system was characterized by "freedom of choice" (in the sense that patients

TABLE 3.2
PHYSICIAN DISTRIBUTION IN NEW YORK CITY, NEW YORK STATE, AND THE UNITED STATES, 1970–1992

	NUMBER OF PHYSICIANS	TOTAL	OFFICE-BASED PRACTICE				HOSPITAL-BASED PRACTICE
			FAMILY/ GENERAL	MEDICAL SPECIALTIES	SURGICAL SPECIALTIES	OTHER SPECIALTIES	
New York City							
1970	20,575	2.61	0.28	0.43	0.39	0.34	1.16
1980	19,184	2.71	0.16	0.59	0.43	0.46	1.06
1990	23,521	3.21	0.11	0.73	0.45	0.47	1.45
1992	25,762	3.52	0.10	0.80	0.48	0.52	1.62
Percentage Change, 1970–92	25.2	34.8	-62.9	85.6	21.8	52.1	40.0
New York State							
1970	35,995	1.97	0.25	0.35	0.36	0.26	0.74
1980	38,451	2.19	0.17	0.50	0.43	0.37	0.71
1990	49,468	2.75	0.15	0.67	0.47	0.43	1.03
1992	53,245	2.95	0.15	0.73	0.49	0.46	1.12
Percentage Change, 1970–92	47.9	49.9	-41.7	109.6	34.9	78.7	52.0

PHYSICIANS PER 1,000 POPULATION

TABLE 3.2 (CONTINUED)
PHYSICIAN DISTRIBUTION IN NEW YORK CITY, NEW YORK STATE, AND THE UNITED STATES, 1970–1992

PHYSICIANS PER 1,000 POPULATION

| | NUMBER OF PHYSICIANS | TOTAL | OFFICE-BASED PRACTICE | | | | HOSPITAL-BASED PRACTICE |
			FAMILY/ GENERAL	MEDICAL SPECIALTIES	SURGICAL SPECIALTIES	OTHER SPECIALTIES	
United States							
1970	255,027	1.25	0.25	0.22	0.29	0.17	0.33
1980	361,915	1.60	0.21	0.33	0.36	0.29	0.40
1990	487,796	1.96	0.23	0.45	0.40	0.36	0.51
1992	520,216	2.04	0.23	0.49	0.41	0.39	0.52
Percentage Change, 1970–92	104.0	63.5	-7.9	122.5	43.0	128.9	57.5

Sources: 1970–90 data from United Hospital Fund of New York. 1992 data from American Medical Association, *Physician Characteristics and Distribution in the U.S.,* Chicago, 1993 edition.

Note: 1990 Census data used for New York City population for 1992 ratios.

TABLE 3.3
PHYSICIAN MEAN NET INCOME BY SPECIALTY FOR THE UNITED STATES
AND MIDDLE ATLANTIC CENSUS REGION, SELECTED YEARS, 1982–1991 (UNADJUSTED DOLLARS)

SPECIALTY	1982		1985		1987		1988	
	U.S.	MIDDLE ATLANTIC	U.S.	MIDDLE ATLANTIC	U.S.	MIDDLE ATLANTIC	U.S.	MIDDLE ATLANTIC
All Physicians	99,500	91,100	113,200	107,900	132,300	126,100	144,700	134,900
General Practice/ Family Practice	71,900	60,300	77,900	78,200	91,500	82,500	94,600	89,500
Internal Medicine	86,800	86,000	101,000	94,800	121,800	126,500	130,900	130,800
Surgery	130,500	133,500	155,400	156,000	187,900	161,800	207,500	186,400
Pediatrics	70,300	58,200	77,100	77,600	85,300	89,500	94,900	98,700
OB/GYN	115,800	101,500	122,700	106,800	163,200	177,600	180,700	160,700
Radiology	136,800	103,700	150,800	153,800	180,700	NA	184,600	156,200
Psychiatry	76,500	76,100	88,600	92,300	102,700	101,400	111,400	105,500
Anesthesiology	131,400	110,200	140,200	133,300	163,100	144,800	194,500	184,800
Pathology	114,400	80,200	127,000	100,100	124,600	NA	131,000	NA

TABLE 3.3 (CONTINUED)
PHYSICIAN MEAN NET INCOME BY SPECIALTY FOR THE UNITED STATES AND MIDDLE ATLANTIC CENSUS REGION, SELECTED YEARS, 1982–1991 (UNADJUSTED DOLLARS)

SPECIALTY	1989 U.S.	1989 MIDDLE ATLANTIC	1990 U.S.	1990 MIDDLE ATLANTIC	1991 U.S.	1991 MIDDLE ATLANTIC
All Physicians	155,800	152,500	164,300	156,100	170,600	171,000
General Practice/ Family Practice	95,900	90,200	102,700	96,000	111,500	100,000
Internal Medicine	146,500	146,100	152,500	144,100	149,600	141,700
Surgery	220,500	209,000	236,400	238,800	233,800	233,200
Pediatrics	104,700	103,400	106,500	91,800	119,300	114,200
OB/GYN	194,300	230,800	207,300	187,900	221,800	260,000
Radiology	210,500	189,200	219,400	237,000	229,800	219,800
Psychiatry	111,700	114,100	116,500	109,100	127,600	126,300
Anesthesiology	185,800	161,200	207,400	195,900	221,100	240,500
Pathology	154,500	NA	172,500	149,000	197,700	NA

Source: American Medical Association, Socioeconomic Characteristics of Medical Practice, Chicago, 1983–93 editions.
NA = Not available.

could choose any available physician), and physicians usually encoun-
tered few restrictions on how they practiced medicine.

For the indigent, the system worked differently. Most could not
afford the fees charged by office-based physicians. Those with no insurance lacked the ability or will to pay the charges; for those with
Medicaid, the fees paid varied among states. (In New York, fees were
well below prevailing charges, leading most physicians to avoid Medicaid
patients.) Consequently, the indigent sought their care at other sites,
usually the emergency rooms or clinics of a private teaching hospital
where residents provided care at no charge in order to gain experience,
or the clinic of a public hospital (also staffed by residents of affiliated
institutions). If hospitalization was required, they would be admitted
and cared for by the house staff as a hospital or "house" patient. For
Medicaid enrollees, the hospital would be paid by the state for each visit
or admission; for the uninsured, care would be covered by hospital phi-
lanthropy or cost shifting to other payers.

Recently, the rapidly rising costs of health care have led both employers and government to seek ways to contain expenditures. This has included purchase of new products developed by the insurance industry—
preferred provider organizations (PPOs) and health maintenance organizations (HMOs). Each type of organization embraces a wide variety
of possibilities, but they represent different types of "managed care."

PPOs are typically sponsored by health insurance companies. They
represent an arrangement between the insurance company and physicians who agree to limit their charges to people covered by the company. The physicians continue to operate from office-based practices, and
patients can choose only from among the physicians participating in
the PPO. Usually, the arrangement with hospitals remains the same as in
standard fee-for-service, with physicians admitting patients to their
selected hospital and the insurance paying the standard charges. Savings
in PPOs are from physicians limiting their charges and insurance companies selecting physicians who practice in a conservative manner, with
relatively few referrals to specialists and hospital admissions. There is
only limited evidence that PPOs provide significant cost savings.

HMOs impose greater restrictions on use of services by their
enrollees. Members select one of the plan's primary care physicians and
receive basic care from that individual. Any referral for specialist care
or hospital admission must be approved by the primary care physician.
These doctors usually have financial arrangements with the plan that

link part of their compensation to the plan's performance, and they therefore have incentives to rationalize utilization. HMOs have demonstrated an ability to deliver care of equal quality at substantially lower costs than traditional fee-for-service medicine, largely by treating more conditions on an outpatient basis.[4]

Nationally, managed care plans have become the dominant form of medical care delivery for both insured patients and doctors. In 1994, fully 65 percent of workers at medium and large companies were enrolled in a managed care plan that limits the choice of physicians compared to 47 percent in 1991, with about 20 percent of the national population enrolled in an HMO, up from 16 percent in 1992.[5] At least 75 percent of all doctors serve at least some of their patients under contracts that permit their decisions to be overseen by insurers; 89 percent of doctors in group practices had some managed care contracts in 1993, compared to 56 percent in 1992.

Expansion of managed care plans in New York City lagged that of the rest of the nation, but these plans are now the way in which about half of all New Yorkers get their care, and the number is rising rapidly. As shown in Table 3.4 (see pages 38–40), combined PPO and HMO enrollment in New York City in 1994 is estimated at nearly 3.7 million, with about 2 million in PPOs and 1.7 million in HMOs. Since the total population includes about 1.5 million Medicaid enrollees, with smaller proportions in HMOs, and many elderly with conventional Medicare coverage, it is likely that a significant majority of working New Yorkers are covered by some managed care plan. No unduplicated count of physicians involved in managed care plans locally is available, but the numbers for each plan shown in Table 3.4 suggest that a large majority of office-based practitioners in the city are seeing at least some patients under managed care contracts.

The recent rise of managed care in New York has three important implications for HHC. First, it will reduce the need for hospital beds in the city. HMOs, and to a lesser extent PPOs, reduce the use of inpatient settings to serve patients by providing incentives to both avoid admissions and lower lengths of stay. This phenomenon is believed to be at least partly responsible for the lower hospital occupancy rates in 1993 and 1994, and the trend is expected to accelerate as managed care plans become even more dominant. A 10 percent reduction in general care bed capacity citywide would represent the closing of nearly 3,000 beds (see Table 2.5); if the cut were proportional in the municipal system, the

TABLE 3.4
NEW YORK CITY MANAGED CARE ENROLLMENT BY PLAN, 1990 AND 1994

	1990 NYC ENROLLMENT	1994[a]		MEDICAID % OF TOTAL	PRIMARY CARE PHYSICIANS	AFFILIATED HOSPITALS
		TOTAL NYC ENROLLMENT	MEDICAID ENROLLMENT			
HMOs[b]						
Health Insurance Plan of Greater New York	735,887	701,318	79,221	11.3	775	25
U.S. Healthcare Inc.	80,790	262,905	30,143	11.5	1,328	89
Oxford Health Plan	59,000	246,400	33,359	13.5	4,600	88
Met Life HealthCare of New York	18,700	103,173	0	0.0	1,447	150
Aetna Health Plans	N/A	100,900	1,446	1.4	3,099	65
Cigna Healthcare of N.Y.	N/A	57,234	2,523	4.4	2,502	105
Prudential Health Care Plan Inc.	20,487	56,739	0	0.0	1,598	35
Sanus	25,575	38,978	0	0.0	1,076	84
Bronx Health Plan	6,081	30,060	29,260	97.3	200	3
Managed Health Care of N.Y.[c]	*	28,297	28,297	100.0	N/A	N/A
Metropolitan Health Plan[d]	3,686	26,972	26,972	100.0	308	9
Manhattan PHSP[c]	N/A	14,878	14,878	100.0	N/A	N/A
Catholic Health Services Plan[c]	*	13,379	13,379	100.0	N/A	N/A
Lutheran Medical Center/Health Care Plus[c]	N/A	10,350	10,350	100.0	N/A	N/A
Health First[c]	*	9,743	9,743	100.0	N/A	N/A
Fidelis Care	N/A	8,349	0	0.0	70	8
Healthnet	77,507	7,870	2,843	36.1	788	50
Managed Health Inc.	N/A	6,101	2,672	43.8	37	8

TABLE 3.4 (CONTINUED)
NEW YORK CITY MANAGED CARE ENROLLMENT BY PLAN, 1990 AND 1994

	1990 NYC ENROLLMENT	TOTAL NYC ENROLLMENT	1994[a]			PRIMARY CARE PHYSICIANS	AFFILIATED HOSPITALS
			MEDICAID ENROLLMENT	MEDICAID % OF TOTAL			
HMOs[b] (continued)							
Prime Care[c]	N/A	5,409	5,409	100.0		N/A	N/A
Elderplan Inc.	5,200	5,043	128	2.5		19	4
ChoiceCare	900	1,886	0	0.0		724	N/A
Physician Health Services of New York, Inc.	N/A	555	0	0.0		471	14
Staten Island Hospital[c]	N/A	376	376	100.0		N/A	N/A
Prime Care Queens[c]	*	304	304	100.0		N/A	N/A
Beth Abraham CCM[c]	N/A	253	253	100.0		N/A	N/A
Travelers Health Network of New York	39,000	N/A	0	0.0		N/A	N/A
Total Health Systems Inc.	35,487	*	0	0.0		N/A	N/A
HealthWays	10,000	*	0	0.0		N/A	N/A
Kaiser Foundation Health Plan of New York	1,200	*	0	0.0		N/A	N/A
Total	1,119,500	1,737,472	291,556	16.8			
PPOs							
Group Health Inc.	N/A	870,717	0	0.0		5,259	187
Magna Care	N/A	530,000	0	0.0		3,572	N/A
Mutliplan Inc.	N/A	360,000	0	0.0		8,500	200

TABLE 3.4 (CONTINUED)
NEW YORK CITY MANAGED CARE ENROLLMENT BY PLAN, 1990 AND 1994

	1990 NYC ENROLLMENT	1994[a]				
		TOTAL NYC ENROLLMENT	MEDICAID ENROLLMENT	MEDICAID % OF TOTAL	PRIMARY CARE PHYSICIANS	AFFILIATED HOSPITALS
PPOs (continued)						
Met Life HealthCare of New York	N/A	176,470	0	0.0	1,447	150
Aetna Health Plans	N/A	13,500	0	0.0	3,099	65
Cigna Healthcare of N.Y.	N/A	6,000	0	0.0	2,502	105
Premier Preferred Care	N/A	2,625	0	0.0	1,826	32
Prudential Health Care Plan Inc.	N/A	865	0	0.0	1,598	35
Total		1,960,177				

Sources: 1990 data from "New York City's Largest HMOs," *Crain's New York Business,* August 27, 1990, p. 30. 1994 data from "Largest Managed Care Networks," *Crain's New York Business,* August 22, 1994, p. 30, except for Medicaid enrollment provided by New York City Health and Hospitals Corporation, Department of Planning Services.

[a] Medicaid enrollment as of December 1994, all other data as of June 1994.
[b] HMO enrollment includes Point of Service (POS) enrollment.
[c] Medicaid enrollment used for total enrollment.
[d] Metropolitan Health Plan total enrollment might actually be higher than the Medicaid enrollment number used for 1994 total enrollment; 1994 total enrollment is not available.
[e] PPO enrollment includes "other" not categorized elsewhere.

N/A = Not available.
* Denotes that the plan did/does not enroll in New York City or that the plan represented an insignificant share of the New York City market and was not reported by *Crain's.*

loss would be about 550 beds—or the equivalent of closing one major hospital. And if all the shrinkage were taken up by the municipal system, its capacity would be more than cut in half.

Second, managed care is altering ambulatory care utilization patterns in ways that may reduce HHC's market share, especially among Medicaid enrollees. Managed care places emphasis on control or "gatekeeping" by primary care physicians, with a goal of more appropriately providing services and reducing unnecessary referrals to specialists. In addition, HMO managed care represents a "lock-in" of patients with the plan they select: use of services by providers outside the plan is not covered. Given the patterns of ambulatory care use discussed in Chapter 2, the growth of private managed care plans serving the Medicaid population will reduce ambulatory utilization at HHC in two ways. Among those indigent now relying almost exclusively on HHC for care, a portion may be diverted to the private plans; among those relying on a mixture of HHC and other facilities for their care, a "lock-in" to a managed care plan will reduce the use at HHC.

HHC represents only about 10 percent of current total Medicaid managed care enrollment, while it represents about 40 percent of all Medicaid inpatient days, a similar share of all Medicaid emergency room visits, and about three of ten Medicaid outpatient department visits. The transition to private managed care plans among Medicaid enrollees will shift demand for services away from HHC, resulting in a loss of market share for Medicaid-financed services.

Third, managed care's emphasis on explicit enrollment (and periodic re-enrollment) decisions at a time when a person or family is not in immediate need of care may change the basis upon which Medicaid eligibles select their providers. In the past, HHC may have been relied upon for care because of the twenty-four-hour availability of its emergency rooms, convenient location in some neighborhoods, and reputation for skilled specialty care through its affiliate staff. These factors remain significant, but in making managed care plan choices, consumers seem to place heavy emphasis on the physical attractiveness of ambulatory care facilities that they use frequently as well as the courtesy and friendliness of professional and support staff at these facilities. It is likely that to maintain (or reduce losses of) market share among Medicaid enrollees, the HHC will require significant capital investment in ambulatory care facilities and a retraining of personnel to inculcate a more "user-friendly" atmosphere.

FINANCING CARE FOR THE INDIGENT

The most uncertain dimension of the future of health care is the nature of financing care for the indigent. The prospects for reform at the federal level have diminished significantly since they peaked after the presidential elections of 1992. This shifts the focus to state governments. While New York State developed a unique system for supporting indigent care under Democratic governors Hugh Carey and Mario Cuomo, the election of a Republican governor in 1994, combined with severe budgetary constraints, may lead to profound changes in that system with important implications for HHC.

THE DEMISE OF FEDERAL REFORM

President Clinton campaigned in 1992 with a promise of national health care reform that would provide access to care for all Americans at a reasonable cost. During 1993, a task force chaired by Hillary Rodham Clinton worked to design a new system and draft legislation to implement it. A bill was presented to Congress at the start of its 1994 session, and it represented significant change.[6]

The Clinton Plan proposed to enhance the Medicare program for the elderly and to provide care for all nonelderly legal residents through one of two mechanisms. For those with jobs, employers would be required to offer a choice of plans and to pay most of the cost (with government subsidies for low-wage employees); the worker would also be obliged to pay a share of the premium cost. For those without jobs, a regional, government-sponsored entity would offer a choice of plans similar to those available to the employed with the financing derived primarily from public funds. All plans would be subject to federal benefit standards, with the mandatory benefits quite extensive relative to prevailing private insurance standards. Cost control was expected to be provided primarily through competitive mechanisms; multiple plans would compete for enrollment on the basis of both their quality of care and price. However, if competitive pressures failed, the federal government was empowered to impose caps on the rate of increase in premiums charged by plans.

An analysis by the consulting firm Lewin-VHI, Inc., found that the Clinton Plan would have had significant fiscal benefits for HHC.[7] The Lewin analysis found that under the Clinton Plan, hospitals that cared for a large proportion of uninsured and Medicaid patients, such as

HHC, would benefit because of the new source of revenue for the previously uninsured and higher payment rates for previous Medicaid patients; hospitals that were heavily dependent on Medicare revenues would have reduced revenues due to the plan's cuts in Medicare payment rates necessary to help finance its broadened benefits. Lewin estimated that HHC would receive an additional $2.9 billion in non-Medicare revenues between 1996 and 2000, but this would be offset by a reduction in Medicare rates, Medicare graduate medical education payments, and the elimination of certain rate adjustments for bad debt and charity care. The net revenue gain by HHC would be $520 million. In contrast, non-HHC New York City hospitals would have lost $3.3 billion over the period, primarily because the Medicare rate cuts would be greater than the additional payments for uninsured and Medicaid patients.

However, the Lewin analysis's generally optimistic findings for HHC should be tempered by some cautionary notes. The analysis assumed that the new coverage of the indigent would not be accompanied by any shift in utilization away from HHC; that is, the assumption was that current Medicaid and uninsured volumes of care would remain constant. Many observers believe that the availability of alternative plans would lead some portion of those now relying on HHC to enroll with a different provider; as this happens, HHC's revenue gains would be eroded. Also, as the analysis noted, the Clinton Plan did not provide federal funding for undocumented immigrants, and HHC believes it now provides a significant volume of care to such individuals. Even under the Clinton Plan, some local source of financing would have been required to support services to the undocumented.

Despite its clear benefits for most indigent citizens, the Clinton Plan, and modified versions thereof, were rejected by Congress. The strongest and most influential objections came from small employers (who feared the impact of mandatory contributions toward the cost of coverage for their workers), from drug and medical equipment manufacturers (who feared that the cost control provisions would cut demand for their products), and commercial insurance companies (who feared premium regulations and a loss of enrollment). Congress failed to devise a politically acceptable compromise. The shift to Republican majorities in the House and Senate after the 1994 elections suggests that the prospects for significant federal reforms are virtually nil for the foreseeable future.

NEW YORK STATE'S FINANCING SYSTEM

The changed federal political climate has shifted attention to the state level as a possible source of reform in health care financing. In New York State, any future changes will be in the context of a relatively sophisticated and highly regulated system that has been developed over the past twelve years.[8]

The origins of the current system can be traced to the late 1970s, when Governor Carey was forced to deal with the aftermath of the bankruptcy of the state's Urban Development Corporation and the near bankruptcy of the City of New York. State budgets were very constrained, and part of the necessary adjustment was a restriction on Medicaid expenditures through a combination of lower eligibility standards and tightly controlled payment rates to hospitals. In addition, Blue Cross payment rates to hospitals were also controlled by the state because Governor Carey felt the resulting lower Blue Cross premiums would make New York more attractive to employers, while wide disparities between Blue Cross and Medicaid rates would provide incentives for hospitals to shun Medicaid patients.

The consequences of these policies were viewed as a disaster by most hospitals. The Medicaid eligibility constraints combined with poor economic conditions, especially during the 1980–81 recession, led to increased numbers of uninsured patients for whom the hospitals received little or no payment. Most hospitals were not well enough managed to keep their costs in line with the tightly regulated Medicaid and Blue Cross rates, and as a result, they also lost money on these patients. The one available recourse was to increase charges for patients covered by commercial insurers, but this soon led to the withdrawal of some insurers from the New York market and a strong political reaction from the others to limit this practice of "cost shifting."

To respond to the adverse impacts on hospitals and commercial insurers, the governor and the legislature devised the New York Prospective Hospital Reimbursement Methodology (NYPHRM). Initially authorized for three years in 1982, it has been revised and reauthorized in 1985, 1987, 1990, and 1993. The current program, known as NYPHRM V, expires at the end of calendar year 1995.

The nature of the NYPHRM system can best be understood by considering separately how it relates to payments for care provided to (1) people covered by Medicaid, (2) the uninsured, and (3) those with commercial insurance. For Medicaid enrollees, the NYPHRM legislation (as administered by a unit within the state Department of Health) determines the rates that the Medicaid program (administered by the Department of Social Services) pays hospitals for inpatient and outpatient care. The inpatient rates are widely recognized as adequate to meet the cost of providing quality care and are set on the same basis as Blue Cross rates, which are also regulated by the state Insurance Department. For emergency room and outpatient department visits, the Medicaid rates are set by the state at levels well below the actual cost of care. Most hospitals accurately complain they lose money on outpatient services to Medicaid enrollees.

New York State is estimated to have nearly 2.1 million uninsured residents, of whom about 1.3 million live in New York City (see Table 3.5). As noted earlier, the uninsured comprise about 9 percent of all inpatient days in New York City hospitals (see Table 2.2), about 29 percent of all outpatient department visits, and about 45 percent of all emergency room visits (see Table 2.3). By definition, hospitals receive no payment from an insurance company for this care, but NYPHRM provides two major indirect forms of payment. First, sums are added to the Medicaid payments to hospitals serving a large share of uninsured patients. These "disproportionate share" payments are partially financed by the federal government and are highly targeted to HHC and other public hospitals in the state.

TABLE 3.5
INSURANCE STATUS OF NONELDERLY RESIDENTS
NEW YORK CITY AND NEW YORK STATE, 1990

	TOTAL	INSURED	UNINSURED
New York City	6,315,413	5,032,635	1,282,778
New York State	15,603,642	13,519,418	2,084,224
New York City Percentage of State Total	40.5	37.2	61.5

Source: New York State Department of Health, *Health Insurance in New York State,* Albany, 1990.

In state fiscal year 1994, a total of about $419 million was paid to hospitals through this mechanism, and HHC received about $349 million.[9] Second, sums are distributed to hospitals to help cover the costs of the uninsured from "Bad Debt and Charity Care (BDCC) pools." These funding pools are created by taxes on hospital revenues from third parties (meaning they are funded by private insurance premiums and Medicaid payments); the pool funds are then distributed back to the hospitals in proportion to their services to the uninsured.

In effect, the BDCC pool is a mechanism for reallocating money from hospitals with a large number of insured patients to those with relatively more uninsured patients. However, the effectiveness of the BDCC pools has been weakened by a diversion of funds from the pools to support programs initiated by the governor or the legislature. In state fiscal year 1994, about $787 million was available in the BDCC pools (these are separate statewide and regional pools); public hospitals were allocated $183 million, private hospitals $448 million, and $156 million was used to fund special projects.[10]

It should also be noted that a third pool mechanism has been created by the state. Hospital revenues from private insurers and Medicaid are taxed to create the pool, and the funds are distributed to specially designated voluntary hospitals (selected because their high volume of service to the uninsured has placed them in financial distress). There are seventeen distressed hospitals statewide, of which ten are in New York City.

With respect to commercial insurance, NYPHRM has sought to make such insurance more viable by limiting hospital cost shifting. The rates hospitals can charge commercial insurers are capped at 13 percent above the rate Blue Cross pays. (The percentage has varied over the life of the NYPHRM program.) While this differential puts commercial insurers at a competitive disadvantage, it is also true that Blue Cross, unlike commercial insurers, has been obliged to offer certain types of policies on which it loses money.

Overall, the NYPHRM system provides the HHC (and other hospitals serving the indigent) with considerable financial benefits. For Medicaid patients, the inpatient rates generally cover adequately the cost of care; for the uninsured, the BDCC pool payments and the disproportionate share adjustments were estimated to cover about 90 percent of the cost of providing their care in fiscal year 1993, but this figure likely was lowered somewhat in fiscal year 1994.[11] It is primarily these NYPHRM policies that have enabled the HHC to reduce its reliance on a city subsidy from about 36 percent of all revenues in 1980 to under 10 percent in 1994 (see Table 3.1), and for the city to reduce its direct appropriation to HHC to $343 million in 1994 from $447 million in 1980.

In light of the state's NYPHRM policies, it is reasonable to ask why HHC still requires a significant subsidy from the city. An HHC analysis of fiscal year 1993 operations provides an interesting answer. Recall from Table 3.1 that, in fiscal year 1993, HHC received a $319 million subsidy from the city and incurred an additional $294 million deficit, suggesting fully $613 million of services were not covered by some type of operating revenue. HHC estimates that the major uncovered item, valued at $214 million, was the difference between the actual costs of its ambulatory care services and the rates paid for these services by Medicaid. The loss due to care to the uninsured not reimbursed by the BDCC pools and other NYPHRM mechanisms was valued at about $45 million. Other major items included a loss on the Emergency Medical Service system of about $73 million, services to inmates of city jails valued at about $48 million, and a variety of services and payments mandated by the city in exchange for the provision of its subsidy.[12]

Restated, the analysis by HHC (which is subject to many caveats and requires cautious interpretation) suggests that HHC still requires a local tax subsidy for three different reasons: First, and fiscally most significant, it provides a large volume of ambulatory care to Medicaid patients, and these services are not adequately reimbursed under the NYPHRM system. Second, BDCC pools and other NYPHRM payments do not fully cover the cost of care to the uninsured. Third, HHC provides citywide services for which either no alternative source of payment is available (care of prisoners) or the available revenues from charges fall short of needed expenditures (the EMS).

What is the future of NYPHRM, and what are the implications for HHC? With respect to Medicaid, the governor's budget proposals for fiscal year 1996 include significant cuts that involve reductions in the rates paid to hospitals for inpatient services. Equivalent reductions are not applied to regulated private insurance payments. A possible consequence of these measures is to make Medicaid patients less attractive to private hospitals, which reduces the access of Medicaid enrollees to those facilities and potentially shifts some inpatient utilization to HHC facilities.

Of greater long-term significance, the governor has requested approval (in the form of a waiver of regulations) from the federal Department of Health and Human Services for Medicaid reforms that would require all nonelderly Medicaid eligibles in the state to enroll in a managed care plan. Implementation of this requirement, which is scheduled over approximately a two-year period, has the obvious implication of effectively requiring HHC and other hospitals serving Medicaid patients to convert promptly to a managed care model in order to enroll their current patients. It is likely that such a mandatory system will lead to some loss of Medicaid market share from HHC to alternative plans and will accelerate the systemwide reduction in rates of inpatient utilization. These forces suggest a need to shrink significantly HHC's inpatient bed capacity.

For the longer term, the implications of mandatory managed care enrollment are harder to foresee. Some return of Medicaid patients to HHC's managed care plan is possible for two related reasons. Evidence from Arizona, which mandated managed care over ten years ago, suggests some new commercial plans may not survive due to poor management. Bankruptcies or closures could suddenly leave patients without a source of care, and they will turn to the public system. In addition, the surviving plans will be subject to cost-containment pressures from the state in the form of decreasing (or only slowly increasing) capitation rates. As lowered capitation rates decrease potential profitability, plans may not market aggressively and may even seek to reduce enrollment. Again the result would be a resurgent need for a publicly sponsored managed care plan.

A final fiscal consideration is the future of NYPHRM's mechanisms for financing care to the uninsured. It is possible that the Pataki administration will recommend eliminating the BDCC pools and likely that funding for care to the uninsured indigent, in whatever form, will become more limited. The implications of these decisions for HHC and the care of the poor are troubling. Losses on current care to the uninsured will increase, and more uninsured patients may be obliged to seek care at HHC, as voluntary hospitals respond to reduced funding by limiting the volume of care they provide to the uninsured.

4.

POLICY OPTIONS FOR THE NEW YORK CITY HEALTH AND HOSPITALS CORPORATION

The Giuliani administration is still developing its long-term strategy for the New York City Health and Hospitals Corporation (HHC), but it has made specific recommendations for the sale of three hospitals. This chapter assesses these proposals in the context of possible broader strategies. It also presents a set of alternative recommendations that would provide a basis for successfully promoting HHC's mission while efficiently delivering services needed by the indigent.

GIULIANI ADMINISTRATION PROPOSALS

As a mayoral candidate in 1992, Rudolph Giuliani offered privatization of municipal hospitals as a health care strategy, but he was vague about how he would apply the concept. A few months into his term, his advisers informally circulated proposals to transfer control of four HHC hospitals (Lincoln, North Central Bronx, Elmhurst, and Queens) to their respective voluntary affiliates and to "spin off" one hospital (Coney Island) as an independent voluntary institution. However, the means of transferring the facilities were not specified (management contracts, leases, and outright sale were all possibilities), and the proposal remained vague.

In the summer of 1994, the administration engaged an investment banking firm, J. P. Morgan, to consider the sale of one or more HHC hospitals and, in late February 1995, prior to the release of the J. P. Morgan report, Mayor Giuliani made a more specific public proposal.[1] The mayor announced his intention to sell three HHC acute care facilities—Queens Hospital Center, Elmhurst Hospital Center, and Coney Island Hospital—and to appoint a blue-ribbon commission to make recommendations for the long-term future of HHC.

The release of the J. P. Morgan report in March 1995 did not clarify the basis for the mayor's proposal. The study asked how much it would cost the city to operate the three hospitals (and no others) over the next ten years and presented an answer of $1.7 billion. But the fact that an agency or facility will require public funding to operate is not by itself a sound reason for selling it. The relevant question is whether and how private operation of these and other municipal hospitals would be better than HHC's potential performance with respect to the criteria of lower cost, higher-quality care, and improved access for the indigent to needed services.

The proposal to sell three municipal hospitals remains vague. Mayor Giuliani stated that the terms and conditions of any hospital sale will be such that "the City can continue its commitment to assuring access to health care services in the communities in which these hospitals are located."[2] But the legal and administrative mechanisms for meeting this commitment in the context of sale of property have not been specified, and the details of their nature are critical to any assessment of the effectiveness of this approach. Moreover, the sale of the three hospitals is not related to a longer-term strategy for the remaining HHC facilities, including eight other acute care hospitals and five long-term care facilities. By asking a new blue-ribbon commission to advise him on a long-term strategy, the mayor appears to be taking the specific step of selling three hospitals without knowing how such a move fits with the broader design for the future of HHC and the medically needy population its facilities serve.

One therefore should ask what the ultimate goals of selling the hospitals can be: (1) Is the sale of these three hospitals a first step toward complete dissolution of the HHC? (Some of the mayor's comments related to his proposal suggests the eventual goal is to eliminate entirely a municipal role in health care delivery.) (2) Alternatively, is the sale of these three hospitals a measure to downsize HHC's acute care capacity in keeping with expected demand trends? The goal in this case would be a smaller public system able to operate more efficiently. In either case, the sale of Elmhurst, Queens, and Coney Island hospitals as a means to achieving these ends can be criticized, each on different grounds.

ELIMINATING HHC AND THE PUBLIC PROVISION OF CARE

The case for long-term dissolution of HHC is that management of its facilities by private (meaning nonprofit, "voluntary") hospitals will result in higher-quality care at lower cost with no decrease in access to services among the indigent and uninsured. The Giuliani administration apparently believes this is a valid assumption. Announcing his intention to sell three municipal hospitals in February 1995, the mayor stated: "We believe the privatization initiative announced today will result in better health care at lower cost."

But the evidence that these three goals—higher quality, lower cost, and equal access—all can be achieved via voluntary management is not convincing. With respect to quality, it should be remembered that voluntary institutions already supply the physicians who provide services at most municipal hospitals; consequently, improvements in the quality of physician services are not a likely corollary of transferring responsibility for property management. Any quality improvements are likely to be the result of hiring more nurses, improved staffing of laboratories and X-ray services, and better-supervised housekeeping. These improvements are not insignificant, and they comprise the "best-case" results of the mayor's privatization plan.

However, greater reliance on voluntary management also is likely to yield *higher*, not lower, costs. The simple fact is that voluntary hospitals have higher unit costs than municipal hospitals for the same categories of service. Here are the figures for two of the institutions being considered for privatization—Elmhurst and Queens—and their voluntary affiliate, Mount Sinai Medical Center, which is widely regarded as a likely purchaser: In 1993, a day of inpatient care cost about $978 at Mount Sinai; the cost at Elmhurst was over one-third less (or $620). At Queens, the cost was $669.[3]

The higher costs at voluntary hospitals are partly due to the higher-quality services, but they also are a function of other characteristics of voluntary management. Nonprofit hospitals not only may have more nursing staff than municipals, they also have more administrators. At

Mount Sinai, about one of every ten employees is in administration; the comparable figure for Elmhurst is 5 percent; at Queens, 6 percent. In this respect, privatization could mean more bureaucracy and higher costs. Moreover, administrators in voluntary hospitals are paid far more generously than their municipal counterparts. The salaries of the chief executives at municipal hospitals are capped at $133,000 annually, and their privileges of office are limited to a car available for business purposes. In contrast, the chief executive of Mount Sinai received a 1992 salary of $580,000, plus generous life insurance coverage and other fringe benefits.

The sale of municipal facilities to voluntary hospitals, if unaccompanied by legal protections or financial incentives, also is likely to reduce access to care for the uninsured poor. A basic difference between voluntary and municipal hospitals is that the former have many "private" patients: These are people admitted by attending physicians who bill patients for their services. (In contrast, virtually all municipal hospital patients are "house" patients cared for by residents-in-training under faculty supervision.) Private patients are essential to the financial health of voluntary hospitals because their private insurance provides relatively generous revenues. Consequently, making their hospital attractive for private patients is a primary focus of voluntary sector managers.

Unfortunately, attracting insured, middle-class patients often means limiting the number and type of uninsured patients who are admitted. The practice is evident when one examines the aggregate figures for "bad debt and charity care," a measure of the volume of service provided to the uninsured. At Mount Sinai, bad debt and charity care represented about 5.5 percent of the institution's total expenditures; at Elmhurst and Queens, the comparable figures were 27.7 percent and 22.4 percent.[4] More dramatic evidence of the voluntary sector's concern for catering to middle-class patients, even to the detriment of others, hit the front pages in 1993, when Mount Sinai was found to be assigning poor (and predominantly minority) maternity patients to rooms with up to four beds each, while privately insured (and predominantly white) mothers were assigned to rooms with one or two beds. In light of many voluntary institutions' incentives to avoid what they view as undesirable patients, it is reasonable to doubt that a sale of municipal hospitals will be consistent with the mayor's intention to maintain a commitment to access to care for the poor.

In this context, it is important to note that existing laws do not ensure all patients access to private hospitals. These hospitals are legally required to treat the poor only in life-threatening emergencies; they have no obligation to continue treatment after the patient is stabilized and no obligation to provide the preventive services or chronic care that many poor children and adults require. For example, a voluntary hospital has no obligation (or incentive) to treat a homeless man with tuberculosis or an uninsured dishwasher with high blood pressure until he is literally on both the hospital's and death's doorstep.

If the goal of selling public facilities to voluntary hospitals is lower cost and equal access, as well as better quality, then it is possible the strategy will not work. It is quite plausible that even if quality rises, costs will increase and access will decline.

At best, the sale of any municipal hospitals should be viewed as an experiment to be evaluated. A mechanism for securing a commitment to continuing access for the uninsured should be carefully designed and tightly enforced. The actual impacts on utilization of care among the uninsured in the community should be monitored, as should the impact on unit costs of services and public expenditures for these services. Only after credible evidence is gathered on the implications of such sales should any further movement toward dissolution of HHC be initiated.

DOWNSIZING HHC

A second interpretation of the mayor's proposal to sell three acute care hospitals is that it is intended to shrink HHC to a more appropriate size in terms of inpatient bed capacity. Under almost any likely scenario, HHC will require fewer acute care beds in the future, and perhaps the Giuliani administration is proposing the sale of three facilities in light of these projections.

If shrinkage of bed capacity is the goal, then it is relevant to ask whether the sale of these specific facilities best serves that purpose. That is, are the right number of beds being sold, and are the hospitals being sold least important to HHC as it continues its mission in the future?

HOW MANY BEDS?

As shown in Table 4.1 (page 54), the three facilities to be sold have a combined general care bed capacity of 1,240. This represents about 21 percent of HHC's total general care capacity.

In fiscal year 1994, HHC had an occupancy rate of 79 percent. The future is always uncertain, but demand trends suggest that, absent

Table 4.1
Selected Characteristics of HHC Acute Care Facilities

Acute Care Facility	General Care Beds[a]	Total Occupancy Rate(%)[a]	Facility Age[b]	Profit/(Loss) (thousands of dollars)[c]	Profit/Loss as a Percentage of Total Expenses[c]	Uninsured Discharges[c]	Uninsured Discharges as a Percentage of Total Discharges[c]
Lincoln Medical and Mental Health Center	614	83.9	1976	$9,745	3.7	2,767	10.4
Metropolitan Hospital Center	392	87.8	1954	($5,573)	-2.7	2,144	12.3
Bronx Municipal Hospital Center	586	75.8	1955	($19,516)	-6.9	4,336	17.0
North Central Bronx Hospital	361	75.8	1977	($8,597)	-5.4	1,720	11.0
Elmhurst Hospital Center	428	83.2	1995	($60,111)	-24.1	3,193	14.2
Queens Hospital Center	385	73.9	1935/1958	($60,260)	-28.6	2,069	12.1
Coney Island Hospital	427	87.3	1954	($35,157)	-19.6	246	1.6
Kings County Hospital Center	858	73.0	1910/1935	($114,685)	-26.5	6,429	20.2
Harlem Hospital Center	623	72.4	1969	($25,036)	-9.2	1,193	6.7
Bellevue Hospital Center	851	76.1	1973	($56,174)	-15.0	4,730	17.2
Woodhull Medical and Mental Health Center	408	84.0	1983	($74,608)	-34.5	1,639	8.8
Total	5,933	79.4				30,466	12.8

Sources: General care beds and occupancy rates from United Hospital Fund, *The State of New York City's Municipal Hospital System,* New York, fiscal year 1994 edition. All other data from the New York City Health and Hospitals Corporation, *Data Book Fiscal Year 1993,* April 1994.

[a] Fiscal year 1994 data (occupancy rates are for all beds); [b] Age defined as the year major portion of inpatient facility opened or underwent total renovation; [c] Fiscal year 1993 data.

any changes, the occupancy rate will decline significantly. If a desirable occupancy rate is around 85 percent, and if inpatient demand is expected to decline between 10 and 15 percent in the coming years, then a shrinkage of about 20 percent is appropriate. Under these conditions, the number of beds involved in the proposed sale seems reasonable. If inpatient demand declines even more rapidly due to a loss of patients to other Medicaid managed care plans and intensified efforts by HHC to shorten its average length of stay, then even more beds might appropriately be sold or closed.

WHICH BEDS?

A loss of about 1,200 beds might be well suited to HHC's future as an efficient organization, and most analysts believe greater savings can be achieved by closing entire facilities than by reducing bed capacity while keeping hospitals open. This is because complete closure yields much greater savings in overhead and support service costs. In this sense, there is a strong logic to the mayor's proposal to sell entire hospitals rather than pursue gradual contraction.

The weakest point in the mayor's proposal is the lack of a clear logic for selecting the Elmhurst, Queens, and Coney Island facilities to sell. If hospitals are to be sold, the selection should be based on three different criteria: (1) the financial impact on the city's taxpayers; (2) the impact on access to care for the uninsured; and (3) impact on future capital needs of HHC.

Based on the first criterion, hospitals with the greatest operating deficit would be the prime candidates for sale or closure. As shown in Table 4.1, Kings County and Woodhull (with a combined bed capacity of 1,266) have the largest absolute dollar losses, well in excess of those of other facilities. Queens and Elmhurst also have relatively large absolute losses, but Coney Island's loss is less than that of Bellevue.

Based on the second criterion, the hospitals serving the least number of uninsured patients (see Table 4.1) would be selected. Coney Island has the least in absolute and relative terms, but Elmhurst and Queens each serve a relatively large number of uninsured inpatients. Selling Elmhurst and Queens is likely to have a greater impact on access to care for the uninsured than would selling, for example, Harlem and Woodhull Hospitals. Moreover, selling both Elmhurst and Queens hospitals would leave the borough of Queens without any municipal hospital, a situation that could add to the difficulties of access to care for the area's residents as well as harm HHC's ability to attract Queens residents eligible for Medicaid to its HMO under future mandatory managed care policies.

The third criterion emphasizes the goal of having a viable HHC in the long term; it suggests selling the oldest facilities in order to have HHC retain a modern plant and reduce future need for capital investments due to renovation. In this sense, Elmhurst is a most unlikely candidate for sale. It recently opened a major new inpatient facility, which is HHC's most modern. In contrast, Queens is second only to Kings County in the age of its major facilities; like Kings County it is in need of expensive renovation. Coney Island is similar to Metropolitan and Bronx Municipal as being among HHC's older facilities.

In sum, the logical criteria for selecting hospitals do not clearly support the mayor's choices. The case for selling Elmhurst seems particularly weak—it is a new facility serving numerous uninsured patients, although it incurs a relatively large operating deficit. In contrast, Woodhull, which the mayor is retaining, serves relatively few uninsured and has a larger operating deficit than Elmhurst. If the mayor's goal is to establish a smaller and more efficient HHC to serve future residents, then his case for selecting hospitals for sale should be made more explicit and stronger. More complete analysis should be done before any facilities are sold.

Recommendations for the Future of HHC

This section presents three recommendations:

1.   There should continue to be a publicly accountable organization responsible for helping to ensure that New Yorkers gain access to needed medical care regardless of their ability to pay.

2.   The public entity given responsibility for this mission should be organized and operated in ways that differ significantly from the structure and processes now established for HHC.

3.   The restructured public entity should make use of competition and concepts of privatization to promote efficiency in its operations.

THE CASE FOR A PUBLIC ENTITY

There is little contemporary controversy over the desirability of the government providing funding for health care of *certain* types. For example, federal payments for the elderly through Medicare and for the indigent through Medicaid are now widely recognized as appropriate. The issue in question is whether, given the availability of public funding for private providers, it is necessary for there to be any public *delivery* of medical care. Rephrased, why could not private organizations replace the HHC if the same funding were made available to them?

Proponents of the position that public provision of hospital care is unnecessary point to the fact that many large U.S. cities have no publicly sponsored hospital. A 1985 survey found that fully fifty-seven of the nation's hundred largest cities did not have a state or local general care hospital.[5] While major cities in addition to New York—such as Los Angeles, Chicago, Atlanta, San Francisco, Houston, Dallas, and Seattle—have a public hospital, others (such as Philadelphia) do not.

The simplest response is that in those cities without public hospitals, the indigent receive less hospital care than do the indigent in cities with a public hospital. That is, having a public hospital improves access to care for the poor.

Measuring access to care is a difficult task, but a widely accepted approach is to use rates of utilization as a proxy for access to care. A comprehensive study of the nation's hundred largest cities found little difference in hospital inpatient utilization rates among the poor covered by Medicaid between the two types of cities, but it revealed significant differences in the *volume* of care provided to the uninsured indigent. Specifically, the rate of hospital admissions among the uninsured poor was fully 40 percent higher in cities with a hospital operated by the local government than in cities without any public hospital.[6]

Virtually every local public hospital in a city is supported by a local tax subsidy, and in virtually every major city without a public hospital, the local government provides no funds to support health care by private hospitals. In this sense, the existence of a public hospital is a real-world measure of the local citizenry's willingness to finance care to the uninsured, and the greater care provided in these communities may be attributed to the availability of taxpayer funds rather than exclusively to the presence of a public entity to provide care. If in a community, and in New York in particular, the local government made available its tax subsidy to private hospitals, would the public hospital be necessary to sustain existing levels of care for the uninsured?

A definitive answer to this question is not possible with available evidence, but some reflection suggests why public provision as well as public funding is necessary to sustain access to care for the indigent. One line of reasoning is purely political. While local public subsidies and local public hospitals may be separable in the abstract, it is very rare for a local government to provide a significant subsidy to private institutions for indigent care. This suggests a cause and effect relationship rooted in local politics; the best way to generate and sustain a local subsidy is to have an identifiable entity with identifiable services and employees who readily justify the expenditure to taxpayers.

A second line of reasoning focuses on the reasons why, even with some local funding, private institutions may be unwilling to provide care to significant segments of the indigent population. As the earlier profile of HHC's services and patients indicated, public hospital patients include large numbers who are unattractive to providers seeking to compete for a largely middle-class clientele. Drug addicts, the mentally ill, AIDS victims, and others are likely to be avoided by many providers even if they are supported by public funds.

A final point focuses on the fiscal realities of local public subsidies for the indigent. Relative to the cost of providing care, local subsidies for the indigent are almost invariably less generous than the federal payments for Medicare enrollees and than the state payments for Medicaid enrollees (which are themselves often below cost). When subsidies are well below costs, private providers are not eager to serve the patients. Only a public provider, established with a primary mission to ensure access to the indigent, may be willing to provide care with sharply limited resources. While the result at public hospitals rather than private ones may be care provided with fewer amenities, and even lower nursing staff to patient ratios, it is only by such measures that available resources are translated into *some* care for the indigent.

The case for public provision of care in New York City rests on the argument that none of the conditions required for adequate private provision presently exist or are likely to exist in the near future. Adequate private provision of care for the indigent requires that (a) local public subsidies be made available as readily to private providers as to a public organization; (b) indigent patients have social characteristics similar to those of middle-class patients for whom private providers compete; and (c) public subsidies for the indigent be as close to the costs of care as are payments for the nonindigent. Since none of these conditions prevails in New York City (or most other large cities), and none is likely to be realized without significant reforms in federal programs, adequate access to care for the entire indigent population probably will require some local public involvement for the foreseeable future.

It is important to add that this case for a public entity is an argument only for *some* public role, not for *all* care for the indigent to be publicly provided. Subsidies should be available to both public and private providers on competitive terms, but a public entity should be available to provide care for those not accepted by or attracted to private providers. If, in fact, the public entity finds itself without patients, then consumer choice would lead to closure of the public facility. However, until that happens, the availability of a public entity serves as an essential safety net for a community. Conditions in New York City suggest it still benefits from having such an institution.

THE CASE FOR RESTRUCTURING HHC

In 1992, the Barondess Commission highlighted two basic structural deficiencies in HHC—its board was tied too closely to City Hall, and the financial relationship between the city and HHC had become dysfunctional because of frequent and unjustified budget revisions imposed by the city. Both structural faults should be corrected in redesigning a public entity to ensure access to health care.

GOVERNANCE CHANGES

First, the board should be made smaller: the current sixteen-member board is unwieldy, does not provide clear policy guidance for the organization, and fails to speak as a strong advocate for HHC's mission. A smaller board (perhaps four or six appointees) selected on the basis of their expertise in health care issues and serving relatively long, fixed terms (perhaps six years) is likely to prove a better governance structure.

The new board should also reflect the state's strong interest—fiscal and political—in adequate care for the indigent. The BDCC pools and other state-controlled revenues are as important to HHC's finances as its city appropriation, and this should be reflected in the board structure. Appointments to the board should be divided equally between the mayor and the governor, with appropriate legislative consent from the City Council and State Senate. The Metropolitan Transportation Authority is an example of a public authority with financing and board appointments shared by the city and state, and this arrangement has helped stabilize its financing as well as provide strong leadership.

FINANCING CHANGES

Much of the instability in HHC's finances derives from the lack of a clear basis for determining the size of the city appropriation. Unlike state revenues, which are "earned" based on the volume of services provided to Medicaid enrollees and of services qualifying as bad debt or charity care, the city's direct payment to HHC is determined almost exclusively on the basis of negotiations with city officials whose objectives vary with the ups and downs of the city's budgetary situation. Clearer rules ought to guide the determination of the size of the city's payment.

Currently characterized as a "subsidy," the city's payment actually serves three purposes: supplementing Medicaid payments for ambulatory care, supplementing BDCC pool payments for care to the uninsured, and funding city-mandated services such as care to prisoners and maintenance of Emergency Medical Services. In each case, negotiations (and there will inevitably be negotiations) between HHC and the city ought to focus on what the city is willing to pay for each of these three types of service; then the volume of service HHC provides would determine the actual amount it receives.

For example, negotiations could focus on the basis of city payment for prisoners (so much per day or per episode of illness); then the amount would be determined by the number of prisoners served. Similarly, the city could agree to a "per visit" supplement to Medicaid outpatient rates or a percentage add-on to BDCC pool payments, and actual service volumes (or the number of otherwise uninsured enrolled) would determine the amount. Such new financial arrangements would let the city set payment levels annually in accord with its budgetary situation but also provide HHC with incentives to earn its revenues.

REORGANIZATION AS AN HMO

A third important element of restructuring HHC will follow from the expected shift of Medicaid to a mandatory managed care model. Medicaid revenues are HHC's largest single revenue source (fully 54 percent in fiscal year 1994), and these revenues will soon be earned largely on a capitation basis rather than a per service basis. A likely corollary is that state BDCC payments and adjustments (if they are continued) will also move toward a capitation model.

Accordingly, *the restructured HHC should view itself and organize itself primarily as an HMO rather than a hospital network.* It should focus on enrolling individuals and families and serving their needs with an appropriate mix of primary and specialty services. Overcoming the historical bias in favor of hospital inpatient services will be difficult, but it is important. Capitation payments provide an opportunity to achieve a better balance between inpatient and ambulatory care, and HHC should aggressively pursue opportunities to increase the share of revenues it receives on a capitation basis.

Effectively managing a system that relies primarily on capitation revenues will also mean reducing HHC's inpatient capacity. As discussed earlier, the move to Medicaid managed care will cause a drop in inpatient days per enrolled person and is also likely to shift some of the Medicaid market away from HHC to other plans. This will cause a significant drop in HHC's average inpatient census, and its bed complement should be adjusted accordingly.

Empty beds should be disposed of, or redeployed. In considering how to make this decision, as well as others that will arise as a result of the changes discussed, HHC's managers should draw upon the useful concept of privatization.

OPPORTUNITIES FOR PRIVATIZATION WITHIN HHC

A policy decision to restructure HHC as a publicly sponsored entity to secure care for the indigent still means that concepts of privatization are relevant to HHC's future. Within a large, multibillion-dollar organization there are and will be multiple opportunities to use different forms of privatization to enhance operations. Four such opportunities are: disposal of surplus bed capacity, developing productivity-based compensation plans for physicians, contracting-out of routine services such as laundry, and competitive bidding by the city for services like inpatient care for prisoners on which HHC now has a monopoly.

DISPOSITION OF SURPLUS BED CAPACITY

Loss of market share and decreasing inpatient utilization rates will create excess bed capacity within HHC. As noted in the earlier assessment of the Giuliani administration proposals, it is reasonable to assume that HHC soon may no longer need about 1,200 of its acute care beds, and that disposing of entire hospitals or larger blocks of beds is the most cost-effective way of implementing these reductions.

Several related decisions will have to be made. Hospitals must be selected and an appropriate disposition chosen. Both the criteria for selection and the methods of disposition vary.

Using the criteria identified earlier, one of the hospitals selected by the mayor is a strong candidate for sale. Coney Island Hospital has a relatively old plant, serves few uninsured, and requires a relatively large subsidy. A case can also be made for selecting Queens; it has an old plant and a relatively large deficit. However, it does serve a considerable number of uninsured. In contrast, Elmhurst is new and serves a large volume of uninsured. A possible substitute for Elmhurst is Woodhull, which serves relatively few uninsured and has a large deficit by absolute and relative standards.

It should be noted that another alternative is to "rent" large blocks of bed capacity to other providers, probably HMOs. Growing HMOs are in need of sites for inpatient services and generally seek to negotiate arrangements for admissions with available facilities. While HHC will face intense competition from other hospitals in similar situations, it could negotiate with HMOs with limited capacity of their own to make available sections or floors of specific hospitals as service units for the HMO's enrollees. The HMO could staff the floors and pay "rent" to HHC for the space. The savings to HHC might not be as great as would result from disposing of entire hospitals, but this approach would permit HHC to maintain a presence in all the neighborhoods it now serves.

The purpose of this discussion is not to select the best option, but to stress that HHC *has* options for how to manage the shrinkage of its bed capacity. Options should be selected based on the policy goals viewed as most important. What is best for improving the viability of HHC in the future may be different from what yields the greatest sale price from an asset.

PRODUCTIVITY-BASED COMPENSATION FOR PHYSICIANS

HHC relies on contracts with private organizations to secure most of its medical staff, and these affiliation agreements represent a form of privatization. Yet these agreements differ from standard approaches to "contracting-out" in important ways: there is no competitive bidding;

performance standards are vague and monitoring weak. Not surprisingly there is much dissatisfaction with the system.

As part of its restructuring as an HMO, the HHC should develop new relations with its physicians that resemble more closely private sector models. Physician staffs at HMOs are typically divided into two categories—primary care and referral specialists. The primary care physicians are assigned enrolled patients and are responsible for managing their care; the doctor's pay is related to how well that job is done. The specifics vary among plans, but primary care physicians usually receive some base pay (a salary or a fixed monthly payment per assigned patient) plus some incentive pay linked to how well the plan has managed to control per patient annual costs. If doctors satisfy patient needs while keeping costs low by avoiding unnecessary procedures, then their pay can be increased. Specialists serving HMO enrollees are available only on referral by the primary care physician and are typically paid on a different basis. They may be paid for their time (per hour or per session), with clear standards of how many patients should be seen in that period, or they may be paid on a fee-for-service basis. In either case, the rate of pay is negotiated between the plan and the physician, with plans seeking competitive offers from multiple sources of specialty care.

HHC should use these models of productivity-based pay and competitive offers to develop alternatives to its current affiliation arrangements. The academic centers that are now affiliates are more likely to be sources of referral specialists than primary care doctors. HHC, either systemwide or by regional network, should identify the volume of each type of specialty care it is likely to use each year and seek bids from different centers for provision of that care. Single affiliations for all services in a region are not essential; different specialty services could be provided by different centers. Payments would be made on the basis of competitively set rates and the actual volume of patients treated.

Recruitment of primary care physicians is likely to require sources beyond the current academic affiliates. HHC should experiment with different types of arrangements, including employing its own physicians as well as contracting with independent group practices and medical school faculty. However, the common element should be linking pay to productivity using some combination of base pay and performance bonuses.

COMPETITIVE BIDDING FOR SUPPORT SERVICES

In a hospital or HMO, physician compensation is only a fraction of total expenditures. Recall that at HHC, the affiliation contracts comprise about 14 percent of all expenses (see Table 3.1). The majority of expenditures are for support staff; some, like nurses, provide bedside care, but many others provide routine services, such as housekeeping, food service, and laundry. HHC has tended to rely on its civil service employees to perform these routine functions, but the work is well suited to competitive bidding for private contracts that could reduce costs.

Laundry services are a prime example of an area in which privatization, through competitive bidding, is likely to reduce costs. The HHC facilities generate about 25 million pounds of laundry each year.[7] The bulk of this laundry, about 17.5 million pounds, is sent to a central laundry facility located in Brooklyn, which HHC established years ago presumably on the assumption there were economies of scale. (The remainder is done by individual hospitals on site; none is contracted out.) However, the central laundry facility has come to be regarded as inefficient. In fiscal year 1993, its operating costs were 57 cents per pound. It is likely that competitive bids from commercial laundries would yield prices well below that figure. Since the central laundry's expenses exceeded $10 million in fiscal year 1993, a 20 percent reduction in costs from competitive bidding would save over $2 million annually. Additional savings might be possible by contracting out the laundry handled by employees at individual hospitals.

Laundry is just one example of the routine services required by hospitals that could be subject to competitive bidding. Cleaning, maintenance, and food service are other labor-intensive tasks the private vendors might accomplish more efficiently than current HHC staff. As HHC is redefined as an HMO with a mission of serving its enrollees (as opposed to a hospital system seeking to sustain its operations), new opportunities for purchasing support services more efficiently than producing them internally are likely to arise.

PRIVATIZATION OF PRISON HEALTH CARE

Caring for the acute needs of inmates of city jails is one important service that HHC provides that is not easily compatible with its restructuring into an HMO. Although the city contracts with a private hospital for some medical services provided to inmates at jails on

Rikers Island, the city relies on HHC to provide inpatient care for its jail population. But these individuals do not fit the model of people who will enroll for extended periods and benefit from preventive services and managed care. Inmates have an average stay in the city jails of sixty days,[8] and they often require hospitalization for psychiatric episodes and wounds or trauma rather than more routine conditions. Almost by definition, their care is episodic rather than of an ongoing nature and therefore not suited to management by primary care physicians.

The HHC estimates the cost of the care it provided to inmates at over $48 million in fiscal year 1993.[9] The services are not separately paid for by the city but are required of HHC as part of the lump-sum city appropriation.

The city should not grant HHC a monopoly on inpatient care for jail inmates. Consistent with the previous recommendations that the city and HHC rationalize their financial relationship, the funds for inmate care should be treated as a separate budget item supporting a specific service. The service should be bid competitively by the city with HHC and other providers eligible to compete. The providers would be asked to bid for specific episodes of care analogous to Medicare's diagnosis-specific hospital rates but tailored to the conditions most frequent among inmates. They would be paid based on the volume of each service actually rendered to prisoners during the period of the contract. It is possible that the city could obtain the services from private facilities at rates below the current costs at HHC facilities.

5.

EVOLUTION OF THE NEW YORK CITY
HEALTH AND HOSPITALS CORPORATION

Public hospitals in New York share a common history with similar institutions in other older American cities. In the nineteenth century, and through the first third of the current century, local governments were primarily responsible for providing food and shelter to the poor. For many years prior to the development and expansion of "outdoor relief," localities fed and housed the indigent at squalid facilities known as "poor houses." When individuals unfortunate enough to find themselves in the poor house also suffered the misfortune of becoming seriously ill, they were placed in infirmaries associated with (and usually attached to) the poor houses. The infirmaries offered medical care provided by volunteer doctors, and later by medical students. These infirmaries for the poor are the ancestors of contemporary public hospitals.

In New York City, responsibility for operating these facilities was shifted from the municipal Welfare Department to a newly created municipal Hospitals Department in 1929.[1] The new organizational status reflected both an upgrade in the priority accorded the service as well as recognition of its enlarged mission.

During the national economic depression of the 1930s, the Hospitals Department's scale of operations expanded to meet a growing need as an estimated 60 percent of the city's population became eligible for care at public expense. Municipal hospitals became overcrowded, and the city launched a major program to purchase hospital care for the indigent from the underutilized voluntary hospitals. Eventually, the city was purchasing care for about one-third of its total indigent patient load from voluntary hospitals (at per diem prices less than the full cost of care), as well as operating a large municipal hospital system at nearly 100 percent occupancy.

During the Great Depression, the reform administration of Mayor Fiorello LaGuardia instituted a number of administrative changes designed primarily to remove political patronage and other corrupt practices from the operation of the Hospitals Department. Employees were placed under the civil service system, purchases of supplies and letting of contracts were subject to careful review and centralized standards, and a central Budget Bureau created in 1933 was given authority to monitor expenditures citywide. Physicians, underemployed during the depression, donated their time for inpatient care and were recruited on a paid, part-time basis for outpatient clinics. Additional physician staff were secured through affiliation arrangements for three hospitals: Bellevue (long a teaching site for the city's leading medical schools) had supervising physicians from Cornell, Columbia, and New York Universities; in 1939, limited affiliations were initiated between Kings County Hospital and the Long Island College of Medicine, and between Metropolitan Hospital and New York Medical College. If New York City's municipal hospitals ever had a period of "good old days," it was probably the period preceding World War II, when it served a large proportion of the population under administrative and medical care arrangements that were perceived as steadily improving, if not fully satisfactory.

THE POST–WORLD WAR II DECLINE

The fifteen years following World War II witnessed a steady decline in the standing of the municipal hospital system. Four major factors underlay this decline.

First, the physical plant deteriorated seriously. Inadequate and overutilized even during the "good old days," the municipal facilities received little new investment during the depression and the war years. After the war some new capital investment was made, but it was directed primarily at building new hospitals, while the existing hospitals, which formed the bulk of the system, were neglected. Between 1950 and 1960, the city opened four new hospital facilities, and this same period was one of major construction for the voluntary sector. Thus, there was a growing disparity between the facilities in the two sectors.

Second, economic and technological forces were working to reduce demand for municipal hospital services, while making hospital care a more expensive product. Group hospital insurance for the working population became widespread during this period, reducing demand for municipal hospital services and increasing occupancy at the newer voluntary facilities. Improvements in the nature of medical care made it a more expensive service as its technological component grew. Standards for nursing care and the need for technical manpower increased, making hospitals more expensive to staff.

Municipal appropriations for the Hospitals Department did not keep pace with these cost pressures. Equipment was not always the most modern, and staffing was often inadequate; nursing and other technical positions could not be filled at permitted salaries, and the municipal hospitals came to rely heavily on less skilled employees such as nurses' aides rather than registered nurses.

Third, changes in the pattern of physician education and the nature of the physician supply made it increasingly difficult for the municipal facilities to recruit and maintain adequate physician staff. Due to tight control by the American Medical Association (AMA) over medical school capacity nationwide, the nation's physician supply did not keep pace with its population growth. Consequently, the 1950s was a period of constant cries of a national "physician shortage."

Given a wider range of choices than they had during the depression, doctors generally chose to serve middle-class patients with health insurance to underwrite their needs. The physicians remaining on the staff of the public hospitals tended to be older men in poorer neighborhoods. The young and generally better-trained doctors followed their more affluent patients to the suburbs and generally did not take on the low-paying or voluntary role of providing care at municipal hospitals. By the end of the 1950s, most of the municipal hospitals were relying heavily on foreign-trained doctors, and several institutions were threatened with loss of accreditation because of inadequate medical staff.

Fourth, the administrative reforms of the LaGuardia era came to be perceived as bureaucratic obstacles to efficient management in the new period of technologically sophisticated medical care. The tight, centralized control over budget and the civil service procedures for staffing led to rigidities in the operation of the hospitals. The Budget Bureau's

system of withholding otherwise authorized funds, designed to cope
with uncertainties, often prohibited hospital administrators from spending them. Moreover, the civil service procedures for defining new positions and hiring new personnel made it difficult for hospitals to establish
required positions and to fill them promptly with well-qualified applicants.
Similar constraints imposed by centralized purchasing procedures made it
difficult for hospital administrators to obtain supplies and equipment in a
timely fashion. Thus the combination of old and poorly maintained facilities, underfunding for operations, a shortage of medical staff, and a series
of inappropriately applied administrative controls led to serious deterioration in the relative quality of services available at municipal hospitals in the
postwar era.

ESTABLISHMENT OF THE AFFILIATION SYSTEM

The deterioration in services at municipal hospitals eventually led to
strong political pressures to take remedial action.[2] In 1959, Mayor
Robert Wagner responded by appointing a blue-ribbon Commission
on Health Services, chaired by David Heyman, an investment banker
active in creating the Health Insurance Plan of Greater New York. The
Heyman Commission reported in July of 1960 and was followed six
months later by a similar effort sponsored by the Hospital Council of
Greater New York. While the two commission reports differed in their
emphases, both highlighted the medical staff problems of the municipal
hospitals, and both pointed to expanded teaching activities and closer
relations with medical schools and voluntary teaching hospitals as a
partial solution to the Hospitals Department's problems.

The commission reports alone did not lead to action, but they identified a path to be followed when crisis struck. The crisis arrived early in
1961 following the failure of Gouverneur Hospital to achieve accreditation (and the subsequent closing of its inpatient facilities) and the
failure of most of the house staff at Harlem Hospital to pass the mandatory examinations initiated in that year for foreign medical graduates.
The mayor appointed a new hospitals commissioner, Dr. Ray Trussel
from Columbia University's medical center, and gave him a mandate to
develop teaching affiliations for each of the city's hospitals.

During his tenure (1961–65), Commissioner Trussel succeeded in
developing contractual relations for professional medical staff for all
the municipal hospitals except Sydenham, a smaller facility in Harlem

to which community physicians admitted private patients, and Sea View, a chronic care hospital on Staten Island. The common element in the affiliation arrangements was payment of city funds on a cost-plus basis (direct costs plus an initial overhead rate of 10 percent) in exchange for provision of services by salaried physicians who would oversee the activities of municipal hospitals' interns and residents. In effect, all of the municipal hospitals (with the above-noted exceptions) became teaching hospitals, and the volunteer and "per session" community physicians who previously provided care were almost completely eliminated from the system.

The specific provisions of affiliation contracts were determined by ad hoc negotiations. By 1965, eighteen separate municipal facilities were affiliated with seventeen different private institutions, including five of the six medical schools located in New York City and twelve different voluntary teaching hospitals.[3] The range of services covered, the process for selection of house staff, and the degree of involvement of affiliates with hospital administration varied considerably. For example, only limited interdepartmental links were established between Columbia's College of Physicians and Surgeons and Harlem Hospital, while Montefiore Hospital assumed responsibility for all professional and auxiliary services, including nursing, at Morrisania Hospital.

The affiliation contracts were generally successful in achieving their initial goal of improving the quality of physician services. Recruitment of staff at the municipal hospitals was greatly eased by the links with teaching institutions, although some of the hospitals affiliated with less well known voluntary teaching hospitals were still obliged to depend heavily on foreign medical graduates.

ADJUSTING TO MEDICARE AND MEDICAID

In 1965, the federal legislation that created Medicare and Medicaid significantly changed the pattern of health care financing in the United States, which had profound implications for the New York City municipal hospital system. The Medicare program provided federal funds directly to hospitals for care of people over the age of sixty-five. The Medicaid program provided federal funds to aid states that provided medical care to persons receiving public assistance and, at the state's option, for people with low incomes who did not qualify for cash assistance but were "medically needy." New York State responded quickly and in 1966 enacted a Medicaid program with a generous definition of "medically needy." Enrollment grew rapidly to reach over 1.9 million, or about one-quarter of the city's population, in 1969.[4] In addition, about 900,000 elderly New Yorkers qualified for Medicare. Given the widespread availability of group health insurance for the employed population, the expectation was that the new programs would ensure that virtually everyone in New York City had relatively good coverage for health expenditures.

For the municipal hospitals, the new programs were expected to be major sources of intergovernmental funds that could eliminate the historical underfunding by the city and provide resources for major improvements in the quality of services. In fact, Medicare and Medicaid did provide substantial new revenues. In fiscal year 1965, the Hospitals Department's budget was $242 million, over two-thirds of which was derived from local tax funds; by fiscal year 1971, the municipal hospitals were budgeting $663 million, with over half of the total from Medicare and Medicaid.[5] These additional funds helped finance the growing affiliation program and permitted expansion of staff and improvement of facilities.

Unfortunately, the fiscal boon from Medicaid and Medicare proved to be short-lived. The large Medicaid enrollments and the program's high costs resulted in cutbacks by the New York State legislature. In 1969, income eligibility criteria were significantly reduced, and only minor upward adjustments were made over the next fifteen years. The initial cuts led enrollment to fall from 1.9 million to 1.5 million between 1969 and 1970. The subsequent near freezing of eligibility levels in the face of rapid inflation caused enrollment to continue to fall for the next decade; by the early 1980s, only about 1.2 million New Yorkers were enrolled.[6]

The pattern of an initially generous Medicaid program followed by a series of cutbacks led the city to launch, and then retreat from, two important initiatives during the early Medicaid period: (1) the creation of a network of Neighborhood Family Care Centers (NFCC) to serve as freestanding sources of comprehensive ambulatory care for a mix of Medicaid and non-Medicaid patients; and (2) a program of expansion and renovation for the physical plant of the municipal hospitals' inpatient facilities. In both cases, however, the initial commitments were not fully abandoned, and they remain an important component of the Medicaid legacy.

In the mid-1960s, the city's Health Department launched a demonstration program to provide comprehensive ambulatory care services in a neighborhood-oriented clinic at its Gouverneur health center.[7] The model was viewed as highly successful in terms of quality of care and consumer acceptance. With the availability of broad Medicaid coverage in 1967, Mayor John Lindsay decided to expand this approach to virtually all of the city's ambulatory care operations. As part of a broader reorganization of city government, the Health Department and Hospitals Department were merged into a single Health Services Administration, the head of the Gouverneur clinic was made head of the new agency, and planning was launched for a citywide network of NFCCs. The plan initially called for thirty-one centers located in all boroughs and was estimated to require a significant new capital investment of about $100 million. Some of the facilities would be at older municipal hospitals whose inpatient services were scheduled for closure or replacement, but most were to be new, conveniently located buildings.

The combination of higher than expected "per visit" cost estimates for the NFCCs and the sharp cutbacks in Medicaid eligibility led city budget officials to argue successfully for reductions in the NFCC program. The notion of separate facilities providing conveniently located, comprehensive, family-oriented ambulatory care remained a goal for the municipal hospitals, but implementation of the NFCC model was limited to a few sites.

The availability of Medicaid and Medicare funds also had led city officials to accelerate and expand plans for construction of new municipal hospital facilities. Major capital projects were authorized for the rebuilding of Harlem Hospital, Bellevue, and Lincoln Hospital; there was to be construction of a new hospital (North Bronx General Hospital) to replace the aged Morrisania facility and to be located adjacent to Morrisania's voluntary affiliate, and construction of a new hospital (Woodhull) to serve central Brooklyn. Since the new facilities replaced ward arrangements with semiprivate rooms (to meet Medicaid and Medicare standards) and included more sophisticated equipment, they also generally required increased operating costs compared to the facilities they replaced. In the case of Woodhull Hospital, the desire to avoid the higher operating costs led city officials to delay opening of the facility for several years, and parts of the completed facility remained unused through the early 1980s.

In addition to their financing implications, Medicare and Medicaid also brought serious, long-term changes in the demand for health care by the elderly and indigent and in the share of that demand that the municipal hospitals were required to meet. In the years following enactment of the federal programs, the number of general care hospital discharges from all facilities in the city rose from slightly over 1 million in 1967 to an all-time high of 1,154,000 in 1972 (see Table 5.1).

For the Medicare population, the new program enabled them to have greater choice among hospitals because they now had coverage and did not have to depend on the municipal hospital system. In the early 1960s, the municipal hospitals cared for about one-third of all hospitalized persons over age sixty-five; by 1970, the municipal share had fallen under 18 percent, and by 1975 to under 13 percent.[8]

For the non-aged, indigent population, the initial impact of Medicaid was also to eliminate the financial barrier to care at voluntary hospitals, but access was still limited because these patients often did not have relationships with the private physicians who generated the bulk of voluntary hospital admissions. Thus, the shift from municipal to voluntary hospitals was less dramatic for the Medicaid population, but the program nonetheless reduced demand for municipal hospital inpatient services. Municipal hospital general care discharges numbered 218,000, or 21 percent of the citywide total in 1965; the figure fell immediately following passage of the new programs but rose again after the state's Medicaid eligibility cutbacks. During the remainder of the 1970s, an industry-wide trend toward fewer admissions reduced the citywide total, but decline in the Medicaid-enrolled population helped stabilize the municipal hospitals' share. That is, the limits on Medicaid eligibility after the early 1970s reduced the number and share of the indigent population enrolled in the program, and the non-Medicaid-covered indigent were obliged to rely heavily on the municipal system. In the 1980s, the New York City Health and Hospitals Corporation (HHC) accounted for about 20 percent of all general care discharges in New York City (see Table 5.1).

THE CREATION OF HHC IN 1969

The enactment of federal Medicare and Medicaid legislation in 1965 coincided with the election of a reform mayor in New York City. John Lindsay had included promises for improvements in the municipal hospitals as part of his campaign, and the availability of new federal financing programs

TABLE 5.1
GENERAL CARE DISCHARGES IN NEW YORK CITY,
SELECTED YEARS, 1965–1993 (IN THOUSANDS)

| YEAR | HHC | | OTHER[a] | | TOTAL DISCHARGES |
	DISCHARGES	% OF TOTAL	DISCHARGES	% OF TOTAL	
1965	218	20.9	825	79.1	1,043
1967	120	12.0	884	88.0	1,004
1970	211	19.4	874	80.6	1,085
1972	218	18.9	936	81.1	1,154
1980	210	19.0	895	81.0	1,105
1985	211	19.0	898	81.0	1,109
1988	203	19.7	830	80.3	1,033
1990	193	19.1	817	80.9	1,010
1991	190	18.3	850	81.7	1,040
1992	188	18.3	839	81.7	1,027
1993	179	17.6	837	82.4	1,016

Source: Compiled from data obtained from United Hospital Fund of New York.
[a] Includes voluntary, state, and proprietary institutions.

appeared to make this goal a realistic one. In 1966, Lindsay appointed a blue-ribbon commission to examine the system under the chairmanship of Gerald Piel. The Piel Commission report in 1967 called for fundamental changes in the local health care system.[9]

The Piel Commission's goal was the elimination of a dual system of health care with lower standards for the poor. The members believed that Medicare and Medicaid would provide the resources to accomplish this goal and also justified a stronger public role in managing the entire health care system. Under Medicare and Medicaid the voluntary hospitals were likely to be deriving more than half of their revenues from public sources, which led the commission to advocate that some public authority should exercise control over all health care institutions in the city. The commission was also concerned about the defects in the operation of the municipal hospitals and sought to improve their management by reducing oversight by the municipal budget and personnel agencies.

The specific vehicle the commission recommended to accomplish these goals was the creation of a new public benefit corporation—the Health and Hospitals Corporation. The authority would be responsible for coordinating all public funds for health care in the city and could use this leverage to establish regional networks of facilities throughout the city consisting of both municipal and voluntary institutions. It would collect third-party revenues and receive a lump-sum payment from the city. The new corporation would also be responsible for operating the municipal hospitals without the constraints of a civil service system or reliance on centralized municipal purchasing agencies. The corporation would be governed by a board of nine prominent citizens appointed by the mayor, none of whom would be employees of the city.

The Piel Commission's concept of a public authority to oversee and coordinate the expenditure of public health care funds did not receive widespread support. Private institutions wanted to retain their autonomy; to the extent that systemwide coordination was to be imposed, the state rather than the city was in a favored position legally and politically. However, improvements in the operation of the municipal hospitals were widely sought, and Mayor Lindsay believed that the commission's recommendation for a public benefit corporation was a way to enhance the management of the municipal hospitals.

In 1969, a political agreement was forged between the mayor, the City Council, and the municipal hospitals employees' union leaders that resulted in state legislation creating the New York City Health and Hospitals Corporation. HHC was given responsibility for operating the municipal hospitals and other health care facilities that the city might assign it. Ownership of the facilities as well as responsibility for capital improvements remained with the city. However, HHC was responsible for collecting all third-party revenues and would be given a lump-sum appropriation from the city. The amount of the city subsidy was set at $175 million in the first year, with subsequent adjustments for inflation and changes in the missions or programs the city asked HHC to perform. HHC was liberated from direct control by the city's budget agency and free to make its own purchasing arrangements. In addition, HHC was empowered to create subsidiary corporations to operate individual facilities, a provision included to permit greater decentralization of municipal hospital operations.

While HHC incorporated some of the structural features recommended by the Piel Commission, the compromises necessary to obtain the authorizing legislation led to several important deviations from the original model. HHC's board was expanded to sixteen people with more responsiveness to the local political establishment than the commission recommended. To gain the support of union leaders, the legislation provided civil service protection for all nonmanagerial municipal hospital employees and retained the municipal employees' union as collective bargaining agent. Informal commitments were also made to limit and eventually reduce the hiring of nonphysician personnel through the affiliation contracts.

HHC went into operation on July 1, 1970, with little lead time for planning. In its early years, it continued to rely heavily on city agencies for personnel, purchasing, and financial management. Since it inherited a weak billing and collections system from the Hospitals Department, HHC was obliged to rely on the city for working capital and found it could not achieve initial targets for third-party revenue collections. Financial autonomy and greater management flexibility proved difficult to achieve rapidly. Because of its numerous early difficulties, HHC was viewed by many as a disappointment. In 1973, a state study commission issued a well-publicized report concluding that "the people of New York City are not materially better served by the Health and Hospitals Corporation than by its predecessor agencies."[10]

Despite its poor image, HHC achieved at least two important objectives during its first five years. First, groundwork was laid for the implementation of improved billing and accounting systems, and collections from third parties were increased significantly. Second, HHC expanded its outpatient services significantly. HHC assumed responsibility for some ambulatory care services formerly under the municipal Health Department and expanded its own efforts. From 1971 to 1975, the number of outpatient visits to HHC facilities grew from 3.1 to 5 million; however, the later year's total includes numerous nonphysician visits, often to methadone-maintenance clinics previously operated by the Health Department.[11]

IMPACTS OF THE 1975 FISCAL CRISIS

In early 1975, the City of New York was revealed to have sizable recurring budget deficits and was denied access to public credit markets. As a result, the city was obliged by its creditors to make substantial cuts in its expenditures, including layoffs of municipal employees. The city was also placed under the supervision of an Emergency Financial Control Board (later the Financial Control Board, or FCB) dominated by the governor. Several semiautonomous or "covered" agencies dependent on city funds, including HHC, were also placed under the scrutiny of the FCB.

The immediate impact of the fiscal crisis consisted of sharp staff reductions and severe expenditure limits for HHC. Its payroll (excluding affiliate employees) had grown from 40,036 in 1970 to 49,080 in 1975; in the next three years it was cut 17 percent to 40,750 and then reached a low of 40,431 in 1980.[12] Total HHC expenditures, which had more than doubled from $475 million in the Hospitals Department's last year to $1,034 million in 1975, were sharply constrained for the next five years and reached only $1,238 million in 1980 (see Table 3.1).

The volume of services provided by HHC was affected only modestly by these resource constraints. Total general care admissions at HHC facilities fell slightly in 1976 and 1977, but in 1978 and subsequent years, they exceeded the total for 1975. However, a citywide and nationwide trend toward reduced lengths of stay meant that HHC's continued provision of care to the same number of people admitted required fewer days of care and hence fewer hospital beds. In 1972 and 1982, HHC had almost an identical number of general care admissions, but average length of stay fell from 11 days to 8.3 days. Accordingly, the number of days of care fell almost 23 percent during this period.[13]

The reductions in lengths of stay and total days of care were accompanied by reductions in the bed capacity of the HHC system.

Between 1975 and 1980, inpatient general care services were closed at five hospitals and the bed capacity of most other HHC facilities was reduced. For all HHC hospitals combined, the general care bed capacity dropped 16 percent, from 7,868 to 6,629, between 1975 and 1980 as a result of closures and reductions in bed capacity at hospitals remaining open (see Table 5.2, page 80).

The fiscal crisis also helped bring about changes in the relationships between HHC and the city government. As noted above, the fiscal monitors established by the state exercised supervision over HHC as well as the city. The procedures developed for financial planning delegated to the city responsibility for submitting a plan from HHC that was consistent with the city's own budget. That is, HHC had to develop a budget that required no more city funds than the city was including in its financial plan for HHC, and this figure had to be viewed as reasonable by the fiscal monitors. The effect of this coordinated financial oversight was to give the city more direct control over HHC budget planning and to make the processes of both subject to greater public scrutiny. After some initial battles between HHC leadership and the FCB, which led to the dismissal of an HHC president in 1976, the city's Office of Management and Budget (OMB) and HHC developed smoother working relationships for arriving at compatible financial plans.

The need to contain spending and the desire to reduce HHC bed capacity also led Mayor Edward I. Koch, who took office in 1978, to seek greater political control over the HHC board and to involve his appointees more closely in the management of HHC. During Mayor Koch's first term this led to conflict with three successive HHC presidents, each of whom served only a relatively short period and left after disagreements with the mayor. This discontinuity in the top management of HHC led to frequent turnover of senior officials and little "institutional memory." Finally, in 1981, Mayor Koch selected, and the board approved, Stanley Brezenoff as president. Brezenoff had served as a commissioner in the Koch administration since 1978 and brought both greater stability and strong loyalty to the mayor to the office of HHC president. Brezenoff was elevated to deputy mayor in 1984, but his successors were people he recruited to HHC and who had served under him. The combination of new board appointees by Mayor Koch and selection of a president sensitive to the mayor's desire to exercise close control over HHC changed the character of

TABLE 5.2
NEW YORK CITY HEALTH AND HOSPITALS CORPORATION GENERAL CARE BEDS BY FACILITY, SELECTED YEARS, 1970–1994

GENERAL CARE HOSPITAL	1970	1975	1980	1984	1990	1994
Bronx Municipal	781	724	656	640	537	537
Fordham	401	406	Closed	Closed	Closed	Closed
Lincoln	350	292	509	517	513	554
Morrisania	331	311	Closed	Closed	Closed	Closed
Coney Island	408	408	378	374	399	399
Cumberland	359	334	310	Closed	Closed	Closed
Greenpoint	174	174	174	Closed	Closed	Closed
Kings County	1,585	1,138	1,008	877	784	808
Bellevue	1,142	828	789	786	806	811
Francis Delafield	261	195	Closed	Closed	Closed	Closed
Harlem	809	793	688	639	540	565
Metropolitan	723	626	522	407	354	359
Sydenham	209	193	120	Closed	Closed	Closed
Elmhurst	651	654	583	493	397	397
Queens	874	673	540	454	377	352
Gouverneur	--	119	Closed	Closed	Closed	Closed
North Central Bronx	--	--	352	347	295	331
Woodhull	--	--	--	322	353	340
Total	9,058	7,868	6,629	5,856	5,355	5,453

Sources: 1970 data from Stuart Altman et al., eds., *Competition and Compassion: Conflicting Roles for Public Hospitals* (Ann Arbor, Mich.: Health Administration Press, 1989), p. 62; 1975–90 data from Charles Brecher et al., *Power Failure: New York City Politics and Policy since 1960* (New York: Oxford University Press, 1993), p. 334; and 1994 data from United Hospital Fund, *The State of New York City's Municipal Hospital System,* New York, fiscal year 1994 edition, p. 29.

HHC from a semiautonomous body to one operating much like other city departments under a commissioner appointed by the mayor.

FISCAL RECOVERY AND PROGRESS AT HHC

In fiscal year 1981, the city achieved a balanced budget, and in the following years, the local economic and fiscal climate improved. In 1981, Mayor Koch successfully ran for reelection with promises to expand and improve services, and subsequently new resources were devoted to most municipal agencies as well as to HHC. In addition, a new state program for reimbursement of hospitals by Medicaid, Medicare, and Blue Cross was adopted in 1982, which provided additional resources through both increased reimbursement rates and special earmarked funds for care for the medically indigent. Moreover, the more stable management of HHC in the early 1980s facilitated realization of many of the collections improvements planned in earlier years. As a result of this combination of circumstances, HHC increased its expenditures 63 percent—from $1,238 million in 1980 to $2,019 million in 1985—and then another 43 percent to $2,646 million in 1989. The share of expenditures derived from third parties increased from 61 percent in 1980 to 74 percent in 1989 (see Table 3.1). Thus, HHC financed its budgetary expansion through both greater third-party revenues and a larger city subsidy.

The new revenues together with a more harmonious relationship with city officials and greater stability in corporate leadership enabled HHC to undertake several programmatic initiatives.[14] Among the more significant were an enhancement of nurse staffing, an upgrading of medical records systems, and a revived effort to decentralize ambulatory care. With respect to the chronic shortage of registered nurses, increased funding was allocated to expand the number of registered nurse positions 29 percent, from 5,098 in 1981 to 6,565 in 1985. However, HHC was not always able to recruit successfully for budgeted positions and had to rely on per diem nurses to meet a substantial portion of its needs. In 1983, HHC created a subsidiary corporation, Nurse Registry, Inc., to serve as a source of per diem nurses and to reduce reliance on overtime and on foreign-trained nurses.

Another chronic problem for HHC hospitals was poorly equipped and staffed medical records units. In recognition of the need for better medical records management for a variety of purposes, including higher-quality care, reduced duplicative testing, and better utilization review,

HHC launched a "medical records initiative" in May 1982. The program provided additional funds as well as attention from central office management to deal with the problem. The passage of a new diagnosis-related system for payment under Medicare provided additional incentives for improved medical records.

The initiative resulted in substantial reductions in the number of incomplete records at most facilities. By 1985, all hospitals except Kings County met the state standard of having at least 50 percent of all records up to date within fifteen days of discharge. Automated chart tracking systems were installed in five acute care hospitals.

Another major effort of the HHC board and staff was to provide better service in its role as "family doctor" to most of the city's poorer residents. In November 1982, the board adopted a formal Ambulatory Care Initiative that called for the reorganization of most high-volume clinics into family-oriented services staffed by primary care specialists and others organized into primary care teams. By mid-1986 this program had been implemented in the general medicine clinics of all acute care hospitals, in the pediatric clinics of ten hospitals, and in the obstetric and gynecological services of nine hospitals. The model was also implemented at the NFCCs. Finally, more accessible primary care was promoted by the creation of smaller clinics at decentralized sites.

The city's general fiscal recovery led to initiatives in the capital as well as operating budgets. Consistent with developments in virtually all municipal agencies, HHC's capital budget was expanded as the city acquired access to public capital markets in the 1980s. A series of biannual revisions to a citywide, ten-year capital plan provided HHC with a promise of major opportunities for renovation. By the time of the 1988 plan, nearly $2.6 billion in capital was allocated to HHC with the goal of building two new skilled nursing care facilities as well as major reconstruction of Kings County Hospital, Elmhurst Hospital, Bronx Municipal Hospital, Queens Hospital, and Coney Island Hospital.[15]

COPING WITH NEW DEMANDS IN THE LATE 1980S

By the late 1980s, the fiscal and public health climate had changed dramatically once again, causing HHC to cope with new demands while resources were curtailed. Like other municipal services, and like many voluntary hospitals, HHC ended the decade beset with numerous problems.

The fiscal difficulties trace their origins to the stock market crash of October 1987. After that traumatic event, growth in the New York City economy slowed as financial sector firms cut employment and suffered reduced profits. The slowed economy lowered expected city revenues and led to reductions in available funds for HHC from the city. In addition, the same slower economic growth hurt the state government's revenues, and the state was not able to fund its health care programs generously.

At the same time that resources were evaporating, new demands emerged for the local health care system. Following a long period of decline, demand for inpatient care increased citywide (see Table 5.3, pages 84–85). After falling nearly 13 percent during the 1980–86 period, general care days rose 2.2 percent between 1986 and 1988. The post-1986 increase in demand was felt most sharply by the municipal hospitals. The number of general care days provided by the system increased nearly 6 percent; the increase in psychiatric care was nearly 10 percent.

One major factor influencing the unanticipated changes in demand trends was the onset of the AIDS epidemic, which resulted in a greater need for inpatient hospital care than was expected. Between 1987 and 1989, AIDS patients in New York City hospitals increased from 1,071, or 3.5 percent of the average daily total, to 1,852, or 6.3 percent, with municipal hospitals caring for a disproportionately large share of AIDS patients.[16] With the emergence of AIDS came the reemergence of tuberculosis, a public health threat that had virtually been eliminated by the 1970s. Caring for tuberculosis patients requires intensive medical therapy and special isolation rooms and equipment. Most tuberculosis control efforts had been dismantled by the 1980s, leaving hospitals and outpatient programs poorly equipped to deal with its reemergence. As with AIDS, HHC cared for a disproportionately large share of citywide tuberculosis patients.

Second, there was an unforeseen rise in demand for psychiatric care, related in part to increased substance abuse, notably the cocaine derivative known as crack. As shown in Table 5.3, psychiatric days increased 22 percent between 1983 and 1988, including a 29 percent increase in the municipal system.

Third, births did not fall as was anticipated by most planners. Obstetric care days rose 4 percent in the 1983–88 period. There was also an increased need for intensive newborn care as the number of low-birth-weight and other problematic infants increased. This too probably was related to greater substance abuse.

Table 5.3
General Care Days in New York City
1980–1988 and 1990–1993

All Hospitals

Year	Total[a] General Care	Medical/ Surgical	Pediatrics	Obstetrics	Psychiatric Care
1980	10,468,894	9,121,979	806,365	540,550	882,829
1981	10,353,004	9,014,578	796,128	542,298	1,019,572
1982	10,359,266	9,038,937	781,067	549,362	1,031,053
1983	10,319,272	8,933,049	777,695	548,528	1,029,586
1984	NA	NA	NA	NA	NA
1985	9,533,670	8,219,713	750,784	563,173	954,236
1986	9,155,085	7,794,676	772,005	548,404	1,176,093
1987	9,298,755	7,958,444	770,390	569,921	1,248,060
1988	9,358,589	8,019,080	767,835	571,674	1,259,295
1990	9,224,609	7,874,222	772,122	578,265	999,161
1991	9,272,965	7,920,809	788,669	563,487	1,118,812
1992	9,051,841	7,756,883	763,064	531,894	1,120,765
1993	8,699,642	7,479,622	704,692	515,328	1,146,405

Percentage Change

1980–86	-12.5	-14.6	-4.3	1.5	33.2
1986–88	2.2	2.9	-0.5	4.2	7.1
1988–83	-7.0	-6.7	-8.2	-9.9	-9.0
1980–93	-16.9	-18.0	-12.6	-4.7	29.9

TABLE 5.3 (CONTINUED)
GENERAL CARE DAYS IN NEW YORK CITY
1980–1988 AND 1990–1993

MUNICIPAL HOSPITALS

YEAR	TOTAL[a] GENERAL CARE	MEDICAL/ SURGICAL	PEDIATRICS	OBSTETRICS	PSYCHIATRIC CARE
1980	1,833,364	1,483,256	215,995	134,113	428,809
1981	1,797,650	1,450,705	208,951	137,994	449,396
1982	1,822,317	1,453,386	222,265	146,666	446,267
1983	1,795,555	1,418,930	222,126	154,899	449,079
1984	NA	NA	NA	NA	NA
1985	1,732,314	1,354,154	217,286	160,874	483,885
1986	1,665,878	1,275,900	229,600	160,288	526,977
1987	1,754,942	1,360,632	230,149	164,161	556,836
1988	1,760,836	1,364,057	233,711	163,068	579,314
1990	1,688,375	1,298,695	232,877	156,803	495,104
1991	1,624,481	1,252,041	230,972	141,468	489,518
1992	1,596,590	1,238,747	220,806	137,037	489,744
1993	1,551,776	1,225,863	177,474	148,439	502,077

PERCENTAGE
 CHANGE

1980–86	-9.1	-14.0	6.3	19.5	22.9
1986–88	5.7	6.9	1.8	1.7	9.9
1988–83	-11.9	-10.1	-24.1	-9.0	-13.3
1980–93	-15.4	-17.4	-17.8	10.7	17.1

Sources: Kenneth Thorpe, "Health Care," in *Setting Municipal Priorities, 1990,* ed. Charles Brecher and Raymond D. Horton (New York: New York University Press, 1989), note 4, updated with United Hospital Fund data.

[a] General Care total excludes psychiatric days.
NA = Not available.

Finally, length of stay did not decline in accord with previous trends and national patterns. The average among general care patients in New York City was 8.8 days in 1988, the same as in 1985. In contrast, the national average in 1988 was 7.2 days.[17] The reasons for the difference include a shortage of nursing home beds, which caused some patients to remain in hospitals while awaiting nursing home placement, but social factors also played a role. For example, the city has unusually large numbers both of homeless patients who are not easily discharged and of abused or abandoned children who also take a long time to place outside the hospital.

These reversals in demand trends were especially problematic because the supply of hospital beds had been shrinking as part of longer-term plans. The New York State Department of Health (DOH) has the authority to regulate capital investments; hospitals cannot build or renovate facilities without its approval. To guide its investment decisions, the DOH developed and periodically revises a plan that is based upon demand estimates for inpatient care. It seeks to balance the number of hospital beds with its estimates of demand.

When these planning efforts started in the 1960s, the consensus was that the city was "overbedded" and that reducing supply would both increase hospital efficiency and permit services to be concentrated in higher-quality facilities. For the 1980s, the DOH expected continued reductions in average length of stay and fewer surgical admissions due to expanded ambulatory surgery. It also underestimated the impact of AIDS. As a result DOH plans called for reduced hospital bed capacity in New York City.

These plans were largely achieved (see Table 2.5). Between 1980 and 1988, the number of general care hospital beds citywide dropped 12 percent. At the municipal hospitals, one of five beds was closed; municipal hospital general care bed capacity fell from 6,629 to 5,241.

The obvious consequence of increased demand and reduced supply is very high occupancy rates (see Table 5.4). While New York City traditionally had occupancy rates above the national average, the discrepancy grew during the late 1980s. Until 1982, occupancy rates in New York City were approximately ten percentage points higher than the comparable national figure. Subsequently, national rates decreased sharply, falling from 76 to 65 percent between 1981 and 1988, while local occupancy rates remained about 87 percent. The city's municipal hospitals experienced the most rapid rise, from 81 to 92 percent. By

TABLE 5.4
GENERAL CARE HOSPITAL OCCUPANCY RATES,
NEW YORK CITY AND UNITED STATES, 1980–1993
(IN PERCENT)

YEAR	UNITED STATES, ALL COMMUNITY HOSPITALS	NEW YORK CITY		
		TOTAL[a]	MUNICIPAL	VOLUNTARY
1980	75.6	86.6	78.9	88.3
1981	76.0	86.5	81.0	87.5
1982	75.3	86.9	82.0	88.0
1983	73.5	87.6	83.0	88.7
1984	69.0	86.9	84.0	87.9
1985	64.8	83.6	80.8	84.4
1986	64.3	82.4	81.0	83.4
1987	64.9	86.6	91.7	86.4
1988	65.5	86.9	91.8	86.2
1989	66.2	85.9	87.6	85.5
1990	66.8	85.5	84.6	85.7
1991	66.1	85.0	81.5	86.0
1992	65.6	83.7	79.8	84.7
1993	64.4	82.0	79.6	82.3

Sources: National data from American Hospital Association, *Hospital Statistics,* 1993–94 and 1995 editions; New York City data from United Hospital Fund of New York, Division of Research, Analysis and Planning.

a Includes proprietary and state general care hospitals not shown separately.

1988, New York City occupancy was almost twenty percentage points above the national average.

A consequence of these extraordinarily high occupancy rates was an overcrowded system. Admissions could not be made from the emergency room because beds were not available, leading to backups of patients in the emergency room. The overcrowded facilities attracted considerable media attention, and the New York City hospital industry—especially its municipal component—entered the 1990s in a particularly stressed condition.

THE BARONDESS COMMISSION REPORT

The strains on the municipal system were becoming increasingly evident when David Dinkins was inaugurated as mayor on January 1, 1990. Between 1989 and 1992, each of HHC's acute care hospitals was visited by the Joint Commission on the Accreditation of Healthcare Organizations (JCAHO), and five of the eleven failed to earn full accreditation. The worst situation was at Lincoln Hospital, which in 1991 received a nonaccreditation recommendation that was not revised until a new survey was completed in 1993.

The public's attention was drawn to declining quality of care at HHC by a dramatic incident in 1991. A stabbing victim in Brooklyn was taken to the emergency room at Kings County and received negligent care—one of his wounds was not noticed and treated— and died. Because Kings County suffered from a long-neglected capital plant and a weak professional relationship with its medical school affiliate, the spotlight was thrown on HHC at its worst. Mayor Dinkins responded by asking a prominent lawyer, Stanley Lowell, to investigate the tragic event. He, in turn, recommended a broader inquiry into care at HHC. In October 1991, Mayor Dinkins, like mayors Wagner and Lindsay before him, turned to a blue-ribbon commission to make recommendations for the future of the municipal hospitals.

The chairman of this commission, Jeremiah Barondess, was a highly regarded physician who practiced for most of his career at a private academic medical center in New York City. He and his colleagues conducted a yearlong investigation. While their report contained twenty-eight separate recommendations, the group's concerns centered on three issues—governance, finance, and affiliations.

With respect to governance, the commission found the HHC board was not exercising policy leadership and was not sufficiently politically independent. City Hall officials continued to direct much of HHC's policy, while the board was spending time on narrower issues and not making key decisions with respect to finances and programs. The commission report's first two findings were: "1. The Board of Directors does not make key decisions affecting HHC, and is not able to provide leadership in quality of care, access, financial and policy issues." and "2. The historical level of city control of the financial operations of HHC has limited the ability of the Board, the President and the Executive Directors to set policy and to manage the HHC facilities." [18]

Because the political links between City Hall and HHC were rooted in the city's financial subsidy of the corporation, the commission
sought a more rational or "business-like" financial arrangement between
HHC and the city. The problem was double-edged from HHC's perspective. If HHC did well in collecting third-party payments, it was
subject to offsetting cuts in the city's annual subsidy. This created no
financial incentive for HHC to seek aggressively higher collections; it
also made state officials feel that more generous Medicaid payments
would not yield improved medical care, but rather would be indirectly
transferred to the city's coffers to help close budget gaps.

In addition, HHC was at risk of budget cuts even if it was meeting
its third-party revenue targets. On several occasions, as the city faced
ever-worsening budget squeezes in the early 1990s, the mayor imposed
restrictions on HHC's budget because the city could not meet its initial
budget commitments for the HHC subsidy. Requested midyear or quarterly budget cuts created turmoil in hospital operations and further
weakened incentives for more aggressive third-party collections.

Mayor Dinkins responded to these financial criticisms by beginning
a process of redesigning the financial relationship between HHC and
the city. A September 1992 memorandum of understanding between
the OMB and HHC set up new rules, which became effective with the
fiscal year 1994 budget. It sought to hold HHC harmless against midyear budget cuts not related to health care developments and permitted
HHC to retain some revenues collected above budgeted targets. While
HHC benefited in some ways from the new arrangement in the last
part of the Dinkins administration, the agreement was not binding on
the new Giuliani administration.

Perhaps because it was created in circumstances relating to poor
quality of care, and because its chairman was a physician experienced in
academic medicine, the Barondess Commission devoted the largest
part of its report to the affiliation system. It found: "A history of mistrust
and fault-finding pervades the current HHC-affiliate relationships and
undermines the ability of both sides to confront the larger issues of
quality of care and quality assurance. This often makes it difficult for
them to move beyond minor issues and to work toward common
goals."[19] The commission blamed HHC for failing to use available
mechanisms to hold its affiliates accountable, but also charged the private affiliates with failing to meet their end of the bargain. "Affiliated
institutions have not in all cases taken adequate responsibility for the

quality of care provided by their staffs in the HHC facilities with which they are affiliated." Furthermore, "affiliated institutions have not always approached their responsibilities for their associated HHC facility with the same level of concern about quality that they show in their own institutions."[20]

To remedy the problems with the affiliations system, the Barondess Commission made several recommendations that together were intended to convert the contested contracts into more mutually supportive partnerships. They urged that all HHC clinical services be covered by affiliation relationships, that these relationships be between executive directors of HHC facilities and their affiliate counterparts, that the municipal and voluntary hospitals participate in each others' planning processes, that the affiliates' other prime teaching hospitals also be a party to the relationship, that residency training at municipal and affiliate institutions be fully integrated, and that an independent affiliation oversight board be established to monitor quality and resolve disputes between institutions. Unfortunately, these recommendations remain largely unimplemented.

It should also be noted that the Barondess Commission considered, but explicitly rejected, privatization as a policy option. The members found that turning facilities over to private management would jeopardize access to care for the indigent. They unanimously advised the mayor: "The Commission rejects the option of privatizing HHC hospitals because it might endanger the city's goals without equivalent benefits."

THE MEDICAID MANAGED CARE ACT OF 1991

While HHC was facing new pressures and limited resource growth due to a downturn in the local economy, the state government was faced with even larger fiscal problems. In the spring of 1991, the state faced a large budget gap for the coming fiscal year, and Governor Mario Cuomo and the state legislature battled long and hard over a series of measures to balance the state budget. Not surprisingly, state Medicaid expenditures were an important part of budget negotiations as an acceptable way to curb spending was sought. The result was the Medicaid Managed Care Act of 1991.

The act required that in New York City and several other major counties at least 50 percent of the eligible Medicaid enrollees be placed in managed care programs over a five-year period. The managed care programs were expected to control expenditures by rationalizing the use of services among the Medicaid population; more cautious use of referrals to specialists and inpatient hospital care would be combined with greater provision of preventive services to lower total costs in the long term.

The city responded to the state mandate by creating an Office of Medicaid Managed Care under the deputy mayor for health and human services. The office is responsible for submitting to the state the required plan for compliance with the act and for encouraging providers to develop plans. The city's Human Resources Administration is responsible for educating clients about the new plans, but plans can enroll Medicaid clients directly.

When the city launched its managed care effort in late 1992, there were thirteen plans enrolling Medicaid clients. However, of these, five were doing so primarily as participants in a relatively small demonstration project in Brooklyn, and four of the five had less than 1,000 enrollees. Two others were also small-scale demonstrations serving a limited elderly population. The single largest plan was the Health Insurance Plan of Greater New York (HIP), which had been serving Medicaid enrollees almost since the program's inception in the 1960s. In 1992, it reported having 48,845 Medicaid enrollees, the majority of all such enrollees (see Table 2.4).

HHC was involved with managed care in only a small way. A demonstration project at Metropolitan Hospital had been converted to a licensed plan in 1985 to serve clients in Manhattan and the Bronx. In addition, in cooperation with a municipal employee union, HHC had established a plan for its workers at Bellevue Hospital, and this was merged with the plan at Metropolitan, known as Metropolitan Health Plan (MHP). In 1992, the MHP had about 4,500 enrollees.

HHC sought to be aggressive in expanding its managed care enrollment but was not successful. Corporate leadership decided to use the existing plan, MHP, as the entity for serving enrollees at all HHC facilities. New leadership was recruited for MHP, approval was sought from the state to extend its service area citywide, and plans were made for marketing initiatives. But implementation was slow, and actual enrollment did not match the ambitions. Between 1992 and late 1994, Medicaid managed care enrollment citywide rose from approximately 80,000 to 292,000. Yet enrollment in HHC's MHP grew only from

4,500 to about 19,600. HHC accounted for only about 10 percent of all managed care enrollment, while it accounted for about 40 percent of all Medicaid inpatient services. Previously existing commercial HMOs, such as U.S. Healthcare and Oxford, recruited Medicaid clients, and new plans such as Managed Health Care Systems entered the market. These HMOs now account for the majority of Medicaid managed care enrollment.

In 1994, new leadership at HHC installed by a newly elected Mayor Giuliani sought to accelerate HHC's managed care efforts. The name of the plan was changed to Metro-Plus, a $1 million marketing campaign was authorized, and HHC hospitals were permitted to contract with commercial plans as a source of patients. This was part of a wide set of issues addressed by the new Giuliani administration.

THE GIULIANI ADMINISTRATION

During 1993, Rudolph Giuliani's campaign for mayor included promises to "privatize" one or more of HHC's facilities. After the inauguration, the administration's fleshing out of these proposals was delayed both by conceptual difficulties and by the press of other events. Most notably, dealing with projected budget gaps focused attention on other, shorter-term issues.

The budget for HHC for fiscal year 1994, which Giuliani's team inherited in January 1994, was out of balance and had been since its adoption the previous June. As part of an election-year strategy, the Dinkins administration and the HHC board agreed to a budget that authorized expenditures that were not fully funded by then-identified revenues. The implicit understanding was that additional funds would be found after the election to close the gap. In its August 1993 review of the city's budget, the state Financial Control Board found: "Our analysis suggests that the city's exposure to an HHC operating deficit may be significant in FY 1994 as well as in subsequent years. In FY 1994, we project that the city's liability may be as much as $150 million higher than planned." [21]

In January 1994, HHC staff informed the new administration that the organization faced an "unexpected" current year deficit of $166 million. The new mayor refused to fund the deficit, and expenditure cuts were imposed. Layoffs and attrition were used to reduce about 1,300 positions, nonpersonnel cuts were made including reductions in affiliate contracts, and some new intergovernmental revenues were found.

For fiscal year 1995, the new administration sought to limit further city support for HHC. Actions taken in June 1994 for the adopted budget and in October 1994 for a revised financial plan reduced city tax levy support to HHC by about $150 million from the agency's baseline. This—combined with growing expenses at HHC—generated a projected fiscal year 1995 deficit of nearly $450 million. HHC still has not developed a complete plan to cope with this gap, but the measures being pursued include aggressive collection efforts and rate appeals to enhance revenues as well as spending cuts. HHC anticipates eliminating about 3,000 positions during the 1995 fiscal year and is using a severance program to help accomplish this. To protect services in the face of fiscal cuts, HHC is implementing a reorganization. Six regional networks have been established to permit downsizing of the central office and consolidation of functions among the twenty-two separate facilities. In addition, HHC plans to reduce staff at hospitals with low occupancy rates and to reduce occupancy in others by lowering the average length of stay for inpatient services. The low occupancy will mean associated staff cuts need not translate into reduced access to care for clients. It remains to be seen how much of the agency's budget-gap-closing plans will be successfully implemented.

The new administration's financial stringency affected capital as well as operating expenses. Early in his new term, the mayor halted work on HHC's largest capital project—the reconstruction of Kings County Hospital. The reason for the action was a belief that the scope of the project was greater than necessary and that supervision of construction was being poorly handled by HHC staff. After a review of the project by an independent task force, its scope was reduced somewhat (primarily by eliminating beds planned for prison health services), and legislation was proposed authorizing construction management to be handled by the state Dormitory Authority rather than HHC. Since the state legislature failed to pass the legislation, the project remains suspended. The Giuliani administration also plans to review other capital spending by HHC.

NOTES

2.

1. This section expands and updates Charles Brecher, "Health," in *Setting Municipal Priorities 1988*, ed. Charles Brecher and Raymond D. Horton (New York: New York University Press, 1988).

2. Merle Cunningham, Jo Ivey Boufford, and Maria Uribelarrea, "The HHC's Ambulatory Care Initiative," in Dominique Jully and Raymond Baxter, *Public Hospitals in New York and Paris*, eds. Victor Rodwin, et al. (New York: New York University Press, 1992), p. 85.

3. Data from City of New York, Office of Operations, Mayor's Management Report, September 13, 1994, edition.

4. Ibid.

5. New York State Department of Health, "Hospital Occupancy Quarterly Report for January-March, 1994," Albany, n.d.

6. Data in this paragraph from United Hospital Fund, *The State of New York City's Municipal Hospital System*, New York, fiscal year 1994 edition.

3.

1. Number of medical schools and graduates supplied by Dr. Charles Killian of the American Association of Medical Colleges. Physician-to-population ratios from the American Medical Association, *Physician Characteristics and Distribution in the U.S.*, Chicago, 1965 and 1993 editions.

2. *Report of the Mayoral Commission to Review the Health and Hospitals Corporation*, New York, November 30, 1992, p. 81.

3. Unpublished estimate by Corporate Reimbursement Services, Health and Hospitals Corporation of the City of New York.

4. See Harold Luft, "How Do Health Maintenance Organizations Achieve Their 'Savings'?" *New England Journal of Medicine* (June 15, 1978): 1336–43; Harold Luft, *Health Maintenance Organizations: Dimensions of Performance* (New York: John Wiley & Sons, 1981); Willard G. Manning et al., "A Controlled Trial of the Effect of a Prepaid Group Practice on Use of Services," *New England Journal of Medicine* (June 7, 1989): 1505–10; Deborah Freund et al., "Evaluation of Medicaid Competition Demonstrations," *Health Care Financing Review* (Winter 1989): pp. 81–97; Deborah Freund et al., "The Performance of Urban Public Hospitals and NHCs under Medicaid Capitation Programs," *Hospital and Health Services Administration* (Winter 1990): 525–46; Ellen M. Morrison and Harold Luft, "Health Maintenance Organization Environments in the 1980s and Beyond," *Health Care Financing Review* (Fall 1990): 81–90; Kathryn M. Langwell, "Structure and Performance of Health Maintenance Organizations: A Review," *Health Care Financing Review* (Fall 1990): 71–79; and Sheldon Greenfield et al., "Variations in Resource Utilization among Medical Specialties and Systems of Care," *Journal of the American Medical Association* (March 25, 1992): 1624–30.

5. "While Congress Remains Silent, Health Care Transforms Itself," *New York Times*, December 18, 1994, section 1, pp. 1, 34.

6. See White House Domestic Policy Council, *The President's Health Security Plan: Health Care that's Always There* (New York: Times Books, 1993), and Congressional Budget Office, *An Analysis of the Administration's Health Proposal*, February 1994.

7. Lewin-VHI, Inc., "The Financial Impacts of the Health Security Act on New York City," Fairfax, Va., April 28, 1994.

8. See Kenneth Thorpe, "Health Care," in *The Two New Yorks: State-City Relations in the Changing Federal System*, ed. Gerald Benjamin and Charles Brecher (New York: Russell Sage Foundation, 1988), pp. 355–82; Governor's Health Care Advisory Board, *Recommendations for NYPHRM V and Related Legislation* Albany, February 1993; and United Hospital Fund, *Health Care Financing in New York State: A Blueprint for Change*, New York, 1993.

9. Governor's Health Care Advisory Board, *Community Health Networks: Leading the Transition to New Systems of Care*, Albany, December 1994, p. 50.

10. The data in this paragraph are from Governor's Health Care Advisory Board, *Recommendations for NYPHRM V*.

11. Health and Hospitals Corporation of the City of New York, *Data Book Fiscal Year 1993*, April 1994, p. I–D–1.

12. Ibid.

4.

1. City of New York, Office of the Mayor, release no. 076-95, February 23, 1995.

2. Ibid., p. 7.

3. Inpatient costs per day based on 1992 institutional cost report data for Mount Sinai and fiscal year 1992 cost report data for Elmhurst and Queens; fiscal year data were trended forward to adjust for six-month difference between calendar and fiscal year costs. Total reimbursable costs for each facility were adjusted to include bad debt and to exclude the following: capital leases; all physician costs; ambulance costs; and medical malpractice insurance for Mount Sinai. Adjusted costs were divided by the number of weighted patient days. Patient days were weighted by acuity to adjust for differences in the volume of intensive care versus less acute services at each facility.

4. Bad debt and charity care data from each institution's cost report shown as a percentage of adjusted costs as detailed in the previous note.

5. Mary G. Henderson, Kenneth E. Thorpe, and Charles Brecher, "Conceptual Model and Methods," in *Competition and Compassion: Conflicting Roles for Public Hospitals*, ed. Stuart H. Altman et al. (Ann Arbor, Mich.: Health Administration Press, 1989), p. 18.

6. Kenneth E. Thorpe and Charles Brecher, "Improved Access to Care for the Uninsured Poor in Large Cities: Do Public Hospitals Make a Difference?" *Journal of Health Politics, Policy and Law* 12, no. 2 (Summer 1987).

7. Data in this paragraph from Health and Hospitals Corporation, *Data Book*, p. II-C-11.

8. City of New York, Office of Operations, Mayor's Management Report, September 13, 1994 edition, p. 35.

9. Health and Hospitals Corporation, *Data Book*, p. I-D-1.

5.

1. This section draws upon Charles Brecher, Kenneth E. Thorpe, and Cynthia Green, "New York City Health and Hospitals Corporation," in Altman et al., *Competition and Compassion*; Charles Brecher, "Historical Evolution of HHC," in Rodwin et al., *Public Hospital Systems in New York and Paris*; and Charles Brecher et al., *Power Failure: New York City Politics and Policy since 1960* (New York: Oxford University Press, 1993), chapter 15.

2. Information on affiliations draws upon Miriam Ostow, "Affiliations," in Eli Ginzberg, *Urban Health Services: The Case of New York* (New York: Columbia University Press, 1970); and Robert R. Alford, *Health Care Politics:*

Ideological and Interest Group Barriers to Reform (Chicago: University of Chicago Press, 1975), chapter 2.

3. See *Community Health Services for New York City: Report and Staff Studies of the Commission on Delivery of Personal Health Services* (New York: Praeger, 1969), esp. pp. 302–17.

4. Kenneth Thorpe, "Health Care," in Benjamin and Brecher, *The Two New Yorks*, p. 363.

5. Brecher, Thorpe, and Green, "New York City Health and Hospitals Corporation," p. 51.

6. Thorpe, "Health Care."

7. This discussion draws upon Charles Brecher and Miriam Ostow, "Ambulatory Care," in Ginzberg, *Urban Health Services*; and Alford, *Health Care Politics*, chapter 3.

8. Figures are from one-day patient censuses conducted by Blue Cross and reported in Joan Lieman, "Federal Financing and Local Control," Ph.D. diss., Columbia University, 1977.

9. Commission on the Delivery of Personal Health Services, "Comprehensive Community Health Services for New York City," New York, December 19, 1967.

10. State Study Commission for New York City, *Health Care Needs and the New York City Health and Hospitals Corporation*, New York, April 1973, p. 175.

11. Brecher, Thorpe, and Green, "New York City Health and Hospitals Corporation," p. 56.

12. Ibid., p. 61.

13. Ibid., p. 57.

14. Brecher, "Historical Evolution of HHC," pp. 73–76.

15. Citizens Budget Commission, *A Review of the New York City Ten-Year Capital Plan*, New York, February 1989, p. 14.

16. Brecher, "Historical Evolution of HHC," p. 77.

17. Ibid.

18. *Report of the Mayoral Commission to Review the Health and Hospitals Corporation*, p. xv.

19. Ibid., p. 75.

20. Ibid., p. 66.

21. New York State Financial Control Board, "The July Announcement, Structural Balance, and the FY 1994 Budget," Albany, August 5, 1993, p. 11.

Index

ABOUT THE AUTHORS

Charles Brecher is a professor of public health and administration at the Robert F. Wagner Graduate School of Public Service, New York University. He also serves as director of research for the Citizens Budget Commission. He holds a Ph.D. in political science from the City University of New York and has written widely in the areas of state and local budgeting as well as health policy. His latest book, coauthored with Raymond D. Horton, is *Power Failure: New York City Politics and Policy since 1960* (Oxford University Press, 1993). In the area of local government's role in health, he is also coauthor of *Competition and Compassion: Conflicting Roles for Public Hospitals* (Health Administration Press); coauthor of *Public Hospital Systems in New York and Paris* (New York University Press); and editor of *Managing Safety-Net Hospitals: Cases for Executive Development* (Health Administration Press).

Sheila Spiezio is currently on maternity leave from her position as research associate at the Citizens Budget Commission. She holds a B.S. degree in nursing from Marquette University and worked as a nurse in hospitals in Illinois and New York before completing an M.P.A. from New York University. After working as an analyst for Empire Blue Cross and Blue Shield, she joined the commission staff in 1993. She recently completed a report for the Citizens Budget Commission, *Modernizing the Municipal Employee Health Insurance Program*, and is coauthor of a forthcoming report, *The Role of Professional Business Services in the New York Economy*.

DATE DUE

Demco, Inc. 38-293